新时代跨境电子商务创新与实践系列教材

跨境电子商务专业英语

总主编　贾如春
主　编　向晓岚　肖　璟　宋　璐
副主编　王敏珊　党　利　康健铭　王子宁

清华大学出版社
北　京

内 容 简 介

本书详细介绍跨境电子商务运营的操作流程，内容紧密围绕跨境电子商务平台的操作运营，系统讲解各大跨境电子商务平台的特点，以及使用英语在跨境电子商务平台进行账户注册、后台设置、选品、引流、采购和发货、订单处理、客户服务、规避常见风险等知识，并通过案例详细解读运营过程中的各种实操流程。

本书旨在帮助读者快速理解常用的跨境电子商务平台的英语术语和背景知识，并熟练掌握跨境电子商务平台的运营技巧，针对性强，方法实用，具有易学、易懂、易落地执行的特点，是跨境电子商务卖家不可或缺的英语操作用书。

本书可作为高等学校国际贸易、商务英语、电子商务等相关专业的教材，也可作为传统外贸企业职员、个人创业者以及从事跨境电子商务运营人士的参考读物。

本书封面贴有清华大学出版社防伪标签，无标签者不得销售。
版权所有，侵权必究。举报：010-62782989，beiqinquan@tup.tsinghua.edu.cn。

图书在版编目（CIP）数据

跨境电子商务专业英语/贾如春总主编；向晓岚，肖璟，宋璐主编. —北京：清华大学出版社，2023.2
新时代跨境电子商务创新与实践系列教材
ISBN 978-7-302-62845-3

Ⅰ. ①跨… Ⅱ. ①贾… ②向… ③肖… ④宋… Ⅲ. ①电子商务－英语－高等学校－教材 Ⅳ. ①F713.36

中国国家版本馆 CIP 数据核字(2023)第 028896 号

责任编辑：郭　赛
封面设计：杨玉兰
责任校对：韩天竹
责任印制：朱雨萌

出版发行：清华大学出版社
　　　　网　　址：http://www.tup.com.cn，http://www.wqbook.com
　　　　地　　址：北京清华大学学研大厦 A 座　　　邮　编：100084
　　　　社 总 机：010-83470000　　　　　　　　　　邮　购：010-62786544
　　　　投稿与读者服务：010-62776969，c-service@tup.tsinghua.edu.cn
　　　　质量反馈：010-62772015，zhiliang@tup.tsinghua.edu.cn
　　　　课件下载：http://www.tup.com.cn，010-83470236
印 装 者：三河市君旺印务有限公司
经　　销：全国新华书店
开　　本：185mm×260mm　　　印　张：13.75　　　字　数：318 千字
版　　次：2023 年 3 月第 1 版　　　　　　　　　　　印　次：2023 年 3 月第 1 次印刷
定　　价：54.80 元

产品编号：093973-01

新时代跨境电子商务创新与实践系列教材

编写委员会

主　任：贾如春
委　员：（按姓氏笔画排序）

王　冲	王　吉	王敏珊	王贵超	韦施羽	邓　茜	邓海涛	申　帅
付咸瑜	向晓岚	向琼英	庄爱玲	刘　轩	刘　潼	刘治国	刘盼盼
江　兵	孙志伟	杜雪平	李　岚	李成刚	李柳君	李晓林	李惠芬
杨　勤	吴岚萍	肖淑芬	肖　璟	潘金聪	何　婧	何智娟	宋　璐
张正杰	陈　方	陈佳莹	陈春梅	陈帅嘉	易　鑫	易建安	罗倩文
周　露	郑苏娟	郑应松	封永梅	柯　繁	钟　欣	钟雪美	段桂敏
祖　旭	胥蓓蕾	莫恬静	党　利	徐娟娟	高　伟	高　雪	郭　燕
诸葛榕荷	黄莹莹	黄善明	董俊麟	雷　瑞	廖　婕	廖品磊
薛坤庆	贾泽旭

专家委员会

主　任：帅青红
委　员：（按姓氏笔画排序）

王　杨	王詩博	包攀峰	刘　忠	刘丁铭	刘立俪	刘永举	李　晖
李　成	李源彬	杨小平	吴庆波	陈梓宇	姚　松	徐　炜	徐　震
曾德贵	蒲竞超	管永林	谭中林	马啸天	朗宏芳	秦秀华

新冠肺炎疫情暴发后,社交隔离、实体零售渠道受阻使全球消费者更深刻地感受到网络购物的便利,线上购物的习惯在后疫情时代或将永久保留,中国跨境电子商务进入历史性拐点,从产品出海时代迈向品牌出海时代。与此同时,伴随着跨境电子商务突飞猛进的发展,贸易规则、平台规则、全球消费市场治理和全球知识产权治理等多重挑战也接踵而至。对于中国外贸企业,尤其是中小型企业来说,跨境电子商务的市场竞争越来越激烈。

英语是全球通用语言之一,了解并熟练使用英语进行跨境电子商务运营操作既可以为中国跨境电子商务从业人员增加新的竞争力,也可以为企业开拓新的销售渠道。

本书以图文并茂的形式系统性地讲述如何用英语在常见跨境电子商务平台进行账户注册、后台设置、选择必备工具、选品、引流、采购和发货、订单处理、客户服务、规避常见错误等知识,是一本帮助读者快速掌握跨境电子商务操作的教材。

本书特点

(1) 本书内容翔实、语言流畅、图文并茂、实用性强,并提供大量的操作实例,较好地将学习与应用结合在了一起;内容由浅及深、循序渐进,适合各个层次的读者。

(2) 本书引用的实例均与电子商务密切相关,例如店铺引流、商品选取、客户服务等,使读者在学习的时候不会觉得陌生,更容易接受,从而提高学习效率。

(3) 理论+实践,提高兴趣。本书的大部分章节都提供实践操作,让读者能够通过练习重新回顾所学的知识,从而达到熟悉内容、举一反三的目的,同时为进一步学习做好准备。

(4) 本书采用案例引导式的写作方式,从工作过程出发,以现代办公应用为主线,通过"提出问题""分析问题""解决问题""总结提高"四部分内容展开,突破以知识点的层次递进为理论体系的传统模式,将工作过程系统化,以工作过程为基础,按照工作过程组织和讲解知识,从而培养学生的技能和素养。

(5) 读者能够通过项目完成相关知识的学习和技能的训练。本书基于企业工作过程,具有典型性和实用性。

(6) 跨境电子商务行业发展得很快,新的平台和交易规则不断推陈出新,本书紧跟最新的业界动态,使内容能同行业发展接轨。

本书符合高校学生的认知规律,有助于实现有效教学,能够提高教学的效率、效益、效果。本书打破了传统的学科体系结构,将各知识点与操作技能恰当地融入各个项目/任务中,突出了产教融合的特征。

  本书由多年从事跨境电子商务研究的行业专家与高校教师共同编著而成,由贾如春负责系列丛书的设计与规划,由刘轩、肖璟、王敏珊、党利等教师共同编写。

编　者
2022 年 12 月

Contents

Unit 1 Overview of Cross-border E-commerce 1

Part A The Concept and Significance of Cross-border E-commerce 2
Part B The Classifications of Cross-border E-commerce 6
Part C The Main Models of Export and Import Cross-border E-commerce 8
Part D The Status Quo and Development Trend of Cross-border E-commerce 13

Unit 2 Main Cross-border E-commerce Platforms 19

Part A Amazon and eBay 20
Part B Alibaba and AliExpress 24
Part C Wish 29
Part D Shopee, Lazada and Other Regional Cross-border E-commerce Platforms 32

Unit 3 Opening a Cross-border E-commerce Store 41

Part A Preparing for Opening a Cross-border E-commerce Store 42
Part B Registering for a Cross-border E-commerce Store 44
Part C Launching Products on a Cross-border E-commerce Platform 54

Unit 4 Marketing on Cross-border E-commerce Platforms 64

Part A Concepts Related to E-commerce 65
Part B Store Description and Product Listing Design 67
Part C Promotion Activities 74
Supplementary Reading 77

Unit 5 Market Research of Cross-border E-commerce 81

Part A Basic Principle and Logic for Product Selection in Cross-border

　　　　　　E-commerce …………………………………………………………………… 82
　　Part B　Practical Methods of Market Research for Cross-border
　　　　　　E-commerce …………………………………………………………………… 85
　　Part C　Data Analysis for Cross-border E-commerce ……………………………… 91
　　Supplementary Reading ………………………………………………………………… 95

Unit 6　Cross-border E-commerce Customer Service(Ⅰ) …………………… 100
　　Part A　An Introduction to Customer Services and Factors
　　　　　　Affecting Customer Experience ……………………………………………… 101
　　Part B　Rules and Features of Cross-border E-commerce Customer
　　　　　　Service …………………………………………………………………………… 105
　　Supplementary Reading ………………………………………………………………… 110

Unit 7　Cross-border E-commerce Customer Service(Ⅱ) …………………… 116
　　Part A　Basic Online Communication Skills of Customer Services …………… 117
　　Part B　Practices of Customer Service for B2B …………………………………… 119
　　Part C　Tips and Templates for Customer Service in Some B2C Scenarios … 126

Unit 8　Policies and Terms on Cross-border E-commerce Platform ……… 132
　　Text A　Various Policies and Common Pitfalls …………………………………… 133
　　Text B　Intellectual Property ………………………………………………………… 138
　　Text C　Appeal and Plan of Action ………………………………………………… 142
　　Supplementary Reading ………………………………………………………………… 144

Unit 9　Cross-border E-commerce Online Payment ………………………… 150
　　Text A　An introduction to Dominant Online Payment Platforms
　　　　　　Worldwide ……………………………………………………………………… 151
　　Text B　Online Payment Platforms in China ……………………………………… 155
　　Supplementary Reading ………………………………………………………………… 157

Unit 10　Cross-border E-commerce Logistics ………………………………… 164
　　Text A　An introduction to Logistics Services …………………………………… 165
　　Text B　Functions of Overseas Warehouses and the Way to Establish
　　　　　　them ……………………………………………………………………………… 169
　　Supplementary Reading ………………………………………………………………… 172

Unit 11 Cross-border Customs Tax (VAT) and Changes in New E-commerce Regulations ·············· 179
　　Text A　An introduction to Customs and VAT ·············· 180
　　Text B　Changes in New E-commerce Regulations ·············· 183
　　Supplementary Reading ·············· 186

Unit 12 ERP and Supply Chain of Cross-border E-commerce ·············· 192
　　Part A　ERP ·············· 193
　　Part B　Supply Chain ·············· 198

参考文献 ·············· 207

Unit 1
Overview of Cross-border E-commerce

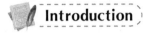 **Introduction**

This unit is divided into four parts to have an overview of Cross-border E-commerce. The first part mainly focuses on the concept, significance as well as the differences between traditional foreign trade and Cross-border E-commerce. The second part is about the two classifications of Cross-border E-commerce. The third part is about the different models of Export and Import Cross-border E-commerce and their respective details. The fourth part includes the status quo and the development trend of Cross-border E-commerce.

Contents

    Part A   The Concept and Significance of Cross-border E-commerce
    Part B   The Classifications of Cross-border E-commerce
    Part C   The Main Models of Export and Import Cross-border E-commerce
    Part D   The Status Quo and Development Trend of Cross-border E-commerce

 **Learning Aims**

- Acquire basic knowledge about the concept and significance of Cross-border E-commerce.
- Know the differences between traditional foreign trade and Cross-border E-commerce.
- Understand the classifications of Cross-border E-commerce.
- Understand the different models of Export and Import Cross-border E-commerce.
- Learn words, phrases, expressions and terms in this unit about Cross-border E-commerce.

Capability Aims

- Be able to talk in English about the basic information covered in this unit

concerning Cross-border E-commerce.
- Be able to understand the differences between traditional foreign trade and Cross-border E-commerce.
- Be able to identify the different classifications of Cross-border E-commerce.
- Be able to identify the different models of Export and Import Cross-border E-commerce.

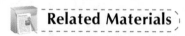

Related Materials

Part A The Concept and Significance of Cross-border E-commerce

1. The Concept of Cross-border E-commerce

With the rapid development and growth of Internet, international trade as well as online shopping and payment, it has made it possible for consumers to shop online anywhere and anytime by reducing potential problems <u>associated with</u> international payments, long <u>shipping</u> time and language barriers.

Currently, customers from all around the world have the ability to purchase products and services that may be unavailable or <u>prohibitively</u> expensive in their home countries or regions from Internet-based platforms in other countries and from marketplaces such as **Alibaba Group**'s Tmall.com that host <u>multinational merchandise</u>. This phenomenon is known as Cross-border E-commerce (CBEC).

Theoretically, Cross-border E-commerce refers to the international business activity where <u>transaction entities</u> from different **customs areas** achieve transactions, online ordering, payments, Cross-border logistics delivery, **customs clearance**, final delivery, and the transaction completion through an E-commerce platform.

To put it simply, the buyers and sellers are based in different countries and the transactions are completed through a Cross-border platform. The products purchased are delivered directly from the sellers' countries or their <u>warehouses</u> in the buyers' countries to the buyers through a series of <u>indispensable</u> processes.

2. The Significance of Cross-border E-commerce

Cross-border E-commerce, starting from traditional foreign trade, develops itself to foreign trade E-commerce, and then the Cross-border E-commerce. Despite its short history, it has been growing rapidly with its own characteristics compared with traditional international foreign trade. For instance, it <u>is less subject to geographical restrictions</u>, less affected by national trade protection measures, and it involves fewer intermediaries. Thus, the prices are lower, and **profit margins** are higher.

Generally, Cross-border E-commerce has a strategic significance as a technological basis to promote **economic integration** and **trade globalization**. It breaks down the barriers among countries, making international trade a trade without borders. Meanwhile, it is leading to the great changes of world trade and economy.

For countries, as a rising form of global foreign trade, it can also stimulate the transformation and update of a country's open economy and establish new economic growth points by providing a country with ways to deal with the new trade patterns. Meanwhile, it has modernized a country's services including logistics, e-authentication, information service and third-party payment. It has also promoted the reform and upgrade of a country's industrial structure.

For enterprises, the open, multi-dimensional and stereoscopic multilateral economic and trade cooperation modes arising from Cross-border E-commerce have tremendously improved the accesses to entering international markets, and greatly facilitated the optimal allocation of multilateral resources and the mutual benefits among enterprises. It can also offer enterprises an effective way to build brands and raise consumers' brand awareness through breaking the **channel monopoly**, reducing intermediaries, saving transaction costs and shortening the transaction period. Particularly, it has created a new development opportunity for small and medium enterprises.

For customers, they have much easier accesses to the information in other countries. They can even conveniently purchase authentic products directly from foreign countries through the Cross-border E-commerce platforms to satisfy their diverse needs.

Questions
1. What does CBEC mean?
2. What factors have led to the popularity of CBEC?
3. What is the importance of CBEC?
4. What are the differences between traditional foreign trade and CBEC?

Notes

1. Alibaba Group：阿里巴巴集团控股有限公司,简称阿里巴巴集团,是以马云为首的18人于1999年在浙江省杭州市创立的公司。阿里巴巴集团经营多项业务,另外也从公司关联的业务和服务中获得经营商业生态系统上的支援。业务和关联公司的业务包括淘宝网、天猫、聚划算、全球速卖通、阿里巴巴国际交易市场、1688、阿里妈妈、阿里云、蚂蚁金服、菜鸟网络等。

2. customs areas：关境,海关境界的简称,也称关税国境,是执行统一海关法令的领土范围。

3. customs clearance：清关,又称结关,指进出口或转运货物出入一国关境时,依照各项法律法规和规定应当履行一定的手续,货物才能放行,货主或申报人才能提货。

4. profit margin：利润率，即公司税后净利润与总收入的比率，一般以百分比形式表示，是衡量公司盈利能力的重要指标。
5. economic integration：经济一体化，广义来讲，是指世界各国经济之间彼此相互开放，形成相互联系、相互依赖的有机体。狭义来讲，是指国家之间通过制定统一的对内对外经济政策、财政与金融政策等，消除国别之间阻碍经济贸易发展的障碍，实现区域内互惠互利、协调发展和资源优化配置，最终形成一个经济高度协调统一的有机体。
6. trade globalization：贸易全球化，是指随着科学技术的发展和各国对外开放程度的提高，流通领域中国际交换的范围、规模、程度得到增强，贸易全球化的前提是技术的全球扩散。
7. channel monopoly：渠道，是指从生产者或服务提供者到用户的过程，如果这个过程被少数人控制，就是渠道垄断。

New Words and Terms

1. shipping	n. 运输；装运
2. prohibitively	adv. (价格)过高地
3. multinational	adj. 跨国的；涉及多个国家的
4. merchandise	n. 商品；货品
5. logistics	n. 物流
6. warehouse	n. 仓库；货仓
7. indispensable	adj. 必不可少的
8. strategic	adj. 战略性的
9. stimulate	v. 促进；激励
10. transformation	n. 转变
11. e-authentication	n. 电子认证
12. third-party	n. 第三方
13. multi-dimensional	adj. 多维的
14. stereoscopic	adj. 立体的
15. multilateral	adj. 多边的
16. tremendously	adv. 极其；非常地
17. access	n. 机会
18. facilitate	v. 促进
19. authentic	adj. 真品的
20. geographical	adj. 地理上的
21. restriction	n. 限制

续表

22. intermediary	n./adj. 中间人;中介;中间的;媒介的
23. transaction entity	交易主体
24. optimal allocation	优化配置
25. be subject to	易受…影响的
26. be associated with	和…相关联

Exercises

Task 1: Complete the following sentences with the words or phrases in the box.

shipping	stimulate	intermediary	access	transformation
authentic	multilateral	enterprise	be associated with	tremendously

1. The company is going to publicize its _____ culture and enhance the quality of its staff.
2. Her interest in art was _____ by her father.
3. One year or two ago, I would have been _____ upset, possibly furious.
4. I don't know if the painting is _____.
5. The packed shoe boxes are then ready to be packed into the _____ carton.
6. The book touches the surface of this question, focusing on binding China into a functioning system of _____ trade.
7. _____ to the papers is restricted to senior management.
8. Jackson acted as an _____ between the two parties.
9. In recent years, the movie industry has undergone a dramatic _____.
10. To generate this key, a password must _____ this ID; however, this ID should not be able to log onto the system.

Task 2: Translate the following sentences into Chinese.

1. Currently, customers from all around the world have the ability to purchase products and services that may be unavailable or prohibitively expensive in the home countries or regions from Internet-based platforms in other countries.
2. Cross-border E-commerce has a strategic significance as a technological basis to promote economic integration and trade globalization.
3. For countries, as a rising form of global foreign trade, it can also stimulate the transformation and update of a country's open economy and establish new economic growth points by providing a country with ways to deal with the new trade patterns.
4. It can also offer enterprises an effective way to build brands and raise consumers'

brand awareness through breaking the channel monopoly, reducing intermediaries, saving transaction costs and shortening the transaction period.
5. They can even conveniently purchase authentic products directly from foreign countries through the Cross-border E-commerce platforms to satisfy their diverse needs.

Part B The Classifications of Cross-border E-commerce

Generally, there are two ways to categorize Cross-border E-commerce.

In terms of business models, it can be classified as Cross-border Retail E-commerce and Cross-border B2B E-commerce.

Cross-border Retail E-commerce includes Cross-border B2C and Cross-border C2C. Cross-border B2C (Business-to-Consumer) is the international business activity where consumers directly purchase products or services from businesses in different customs areas through an E-commerce platform. This international activity involves the processes of transaction concluding, payment completion and settlement, product delivery through Cross-border logistics and transaction completion. Cross-border C2C (Consumer-to-Consumer) is the international business activity where individual buyers purchase products or services from individual sellers in different customs areas through a third-party E-commerce platform. Individual buyers can browse all the information about the products published by the sellers on the platform.

Cross-border B2B (Business-to-Business) E-commerce is the international business activity between businesses from different customs areas. This international activity involves the processes of transaction concluding, payment completion and settlement through an E-commerce platform, product delivery through Cross-border logistics and transaction completion.

In terms of customs areas, it can be classified as Export Cross-border E-commerce and Import Cross-border E-commerce.

Export Cross-border E-commerce is that the foreign consumers visit the shopping platforms of domestic sellers to select goods. After placing the order and completing the payment, the goods are delivered by the domestic sellers to logistics for shipment. After the two countries' customs clearance and **commodity inspection**, the goods are finally delivered to the foreign consumers.

While Import Cross-border E-commerce refers to the fact that the domestic consumers visit the shopping platforms of the foreign sellers to select goods. After placing the order and completing the payment, the goods are delivered by the foreign sellers to logistics for shipment. After the two countries' customs clearance and commodity inspection, the goods are finally delivered to the domestic consumers.

Some Cross-border sellers directly cooperate with a third-party platform, and the third-party platform is responsible for all the processes like logistics, customs clearance and commodity inspection.

Questions

1. How many ways are there to classify CBEC?
2. What does B2B mean?
3. What are the two business models of Cross-border E-commerce?

Notes

commodity inspection：商品检验，是指商品的产方、买方或者第三方在一定条件下，借助于某种手段和方法，按照合同、标准或国内外相关法律、法规、惯例，对商品的质量、规格、重量、数量、包装、安全及卫生等方面进行检查，并做出合格与否或验收通过与否的判定。

New Words and Terms

1. categorize	v. 分类
2. classify	v. 分类
3. retail	n./v. 零售
4. settlement	n. 结算
5. browse	v. 浏览
6. publish	v. 发表；公布
7. shipment	n. 运输；装运
8. in terms of	从…方面；就…而言
9. conclude a transaction	达成交易
10. place the order	下订单
11. commodity inspection	商品检验

Exercises

Task 3：Complete the following sentences with the words or phrases in the box.

classify	settlement	publish	retail	browse	third party

1. The report will be _____ on the Internet.
2. You are welcome to come in and _____.
3. The books in the library are _____ according to subject.

4. He is a manager with twenty years' experience in the _____ business.
5. These are reasons why the US dollar is often used for payment and _____ of international trade between non-US economies.
6. Party B is not allowed to subcontract the design work completely or partially to any _____ without the permission of Party A.

Task 4: Translate the following sentences into Chinese.

1. Cross-border B2C (Business-to-Consumer) is the international business activity where consumers directly purchase products or services from businesses in different customs areas through an E-commerce platform.
2. This international activity involves the processes of transaction concluding, payment completion and settlement through an E-commerce platform, product delivery through Cross-border logistics and transaction completion.
3. After placing the order and completing the payment, the goods are delivered by the domestic sellers to logistics for shipment.
4. While import Cross-border E-commerce refers to the fact that domestic consumers visit the shopping platforms of the foreign sellers to select goods.
5. Some Cross-border sellers directly cooperate with a third-party platform, and the third-party platform is responsible for logistics, customs clearance and commodity inspection.

Part C The Main Models of Export and Import Cross-border E-commerce

Both Export Cross-border E-commerce and Import Cross-border E-commerce have various models.

1. The Main Models of Export Cross-border E-commerce

For Export Cross-border E-commerce, it mainly includes two models: B2B and B2C/C2C.

For B2B, it is further divided into information service platforms and transaction service platforms. The information service platforms mainly achieve the services of transaction completion through a third-party platform by distributing and searching information. **Alibaba International Station**, **Toocle** and **Global Sources** are representative platforms. While the transaction service platforms build a platform business mode that can realize the online trading and payment for both the supply and the purchasing parties. **DHgate** and **OSell** are representative platforms.

For B2C/C2C, it is sorted into open platforms and self-operated platforms. The open platforms achieve the systematic docking of applications and platforms, and build an ecosystem itself based on the platform. The representative platforms are **Amazon**, **Wish**, **AliExpress**, and other big platforms like **eBay** or small-scale platforms like **Lazada**. While the self-operated platforms have a unified management of all the products on the platform, including the product display, online trading as well as commodity delivery to the consumers through logistics. **Globalegrow** and **LightInTheBox** are the representative platforms.

2. The Main Models of Import Cross-border E-commerce

For Import Cross-border E-commerce, it mainly includes three models: **bonded area** import model, oversea direct mail import model and express customs clearance model.

For bonded area import model, the representative platform is Jumei. Under this mode, Cross-border E-commerce enterprises purchase products in bulk from overseas and the products are shipped and stored in the domestic bonded areas. When the consumers place orders in the E-commerce platforms, the orders, payment information and logistics information are sent real-time to the Customs and related supervision departments. Then all the customs clearance processes like declaration, taxation and inspection will be completed. Finally, these Cross-border commodities will be delivered directly from the warehouses in the bonded areas through domestic logistics to the consumers.

For overseas direct mail import model, the representative platform is Amazon. Under this mode, after consumers place orders in Cross-border E-commerce platforms, E-commerce enterprises or declaration enterprises declare through the Cross-border E-commerce system. Meanwhile, the E-commerce enterprises or declaration enterprises send information about orders, payment and logistics to the Customs. After the Cross-border E-commerce system completes all the information, the Cross-border goods will be packed in the overseas warehouses and enter a country in the form of individual packages. When the goods enter a country, processes like inspection, taxation and customs clearance will be completed under the Customs and other departments. Finally, the Cross-border goods will be delivered through domestic logistics to the consumers. The features of this mode are the global premium supply chain logistics system and substantial **SKU**(Stock Keeping Unit)s.

For express customs clearance model, after the orders are confirmed, the overseas suppliers directly mail the goods to the consumers from abroad through international express delivery without the customs documents. The feature of this model is flexible with no need to prepare goods in advance. Therefore, it is suitable for the phase of few transactions and orders.

Questions

1. What are the major models of Export Cross-border E-commerce?
2. What are the major models of Import Cross-border E-commerce?
3. What is information service platform?
4. What are self-operated platforms?
5. What are the features of oversea direct mail import model?

Notes

1. Alibaba International Station：阿里巴巴国际站,旨在帮助中小企业拓展国际贸易的出口营销推广业务,基于全球领先的企业间电子商务网站阿里巴巴国际站贸易平台,通过向海外买家展示、推广供应商的企业和产品,进而获得贸易商机和订单,是出口企业拓展国际贸易的网络平台之一。

2. Toocle：浙江网盛生意宝股份有限公司,简称生意宝,是一家专业从事互联网信息服务、电子商务和企业应用软件开发的高科技企业,是国内规模较大的垂直专业网站开发运营商,专业 B2B 电子商务标志性企业。

3. Global Sources：环球资源,是一家扎根中国香港,面向全球的专业展览主办机构,旗下的环球资源网站是深度行业化的专业 B2B 外贸平台,更是中国商务部主办的《国际商报》多次发文点名认可的全球高端买家的采购平台、主流平台,一直致力于促成国际贸易,并通过展会、数字化贸易平台及贸易杂志等多种渠道连接全球诚信买家及已核实的供应商,并提供定制化的采购方案及值得信赖的市场资讯。

4. DHgate：敦煌网,全球领先的在线外贸交易平台,致力于帮助中国的中小企业通过跨境电子商务平台走向全球市场,开辟一条全新的国际贸易通道,让在线交易变得更加简单、安全、高效,是国内首个为中小企业提供 B2B 网上交易平台的网站;它采用佣金制,只在买卖双方交易成功后收取费用。

5. OSell：约商,全球首款跨境贸易商务社交 APP,是为全球商人提供的一款即时通信类的商务社交移动应用,旨在让不同国家的商人都能使用母语随时对话;约商以解决各国商人的沟通交流为核心,同时提供商人按需配对、高度整合的外贸市场、全球布局的精品体验馆等服务,真正实现全球商人交流、交易无障碍。

6. Amazon：亚马逊,美国规模最大的电子商务公司,位于华盛顿州的西雅图,是网络上最早一批开始经营电子商务的公司之一,成立于 1994 年,一开始只经营网络书籍销售业务,现在扩大到范围广泛的其他产品,已成为全球商品品种最多的网上零售商和全球第二大互联网企业。

7. Wish：一款专注于移动购物的跨境 B2C 电商平台;平台根据用户喜好,通过精确的算法推荐技术将商品信息推送给感兴趣的用户,主张以亲民的价格给消费者提供优质的产品。

8. AliExpress：全球速卖通,阿里巴巴旗下的面向国际市场的跨境电商平台,被广大卖家称为国际版淘宝,面向海外买家客户,通过支付宝国际账户进行担保交易,并使用国际物流渠道运输发货,是全球第三大英文在线购物网站。

9. eBay：电子湾，又称易贝，是一个可让全球用户上网买卖物品的线上拍卖及购物网站，于 1995 年成立于加利福尼亚州圣荷塞，用户可以在 eBay 上通过网络出售商品。
10. Lazada：来赞达，东南亚地区最大的在线购物网站，目标市场是印度尼西亚、马来西亚、菲律宾以及泰国。
11. Globalegrow：深圳市环球易购电子商务有限公司，创建于 2007 年，是一家跨境 B2C 电子商务平台，始终走在全球电子商务一体化时代的前沿，专注于经营休闲服装、电子产品、婚纱礼服、手表、玩具等多个垂直品类的跨境出口零售服务。
12. LightInTheBox：兰亭集势，简称兰亭，是以技术驱动、大数据为贯穿点，整合供应链生态圈服务的在线 B2C 跨境电商公司；One World One Market 是兰亭集势的使命，即为全世界中小零售商提供一个基于互联网的全球整合供应链。
13. bonded area：也称保税仓库区，级别低于综合保税区，是指由一国海关设置的或经海关批准注册、受海关监督和管理的可以长时间存放商品的区域。
14. SKU（Stock Keeping Unit）：库存保有单位，即库存进出计量的单位，可以件、盒、托盘等为单位。

New Words and Terms

1.	distribute	v. 分配
2.	representative	adj. 代表性的
3.	sort	v. 分类
4.	self-operated	adj. 自营的
5.	application	n. 应用
6.	ecosystem	n. 生态圈
7.	small-scale	adj. 小规模的
8.	unified	adj. 统一的
9.	supervision	n. 监管
10.	taxation	n. 征税
11.	premium	adj. 优质的
12.	substantial	adj. 大量的
13.	confirm	v. 确认
14.	supplier	n. 供应商
15.	flexible	adj. 灵活的
16.	phase	n. 阶段
17.	systematic docking	系统化对接
18.	in bulk	大批量

续表

19. the Customs	海关部门
20. customs documents	海关单据

Exercises

Task 5: Complete the following sentences with the words or phrases in the box.

distribute	supplier	sort	in bulk	substantial
taxation	premium	confirm	supervision	representative

1. Costumes and sets were also made under his _____.
2. That company is the UK's largest _____ of office equipment.
3. Due to the international nature of aircraft operations, airline operators are more susceptible to double _____ than other taxpayers.
4. The painting is not _____ of his work of the period.
5. The eggs are _____ according to size.
6. Clothes and blankets have been _____ among the refugees.
7. China is one of the top markets for _____ car brands.
8. We have the support of a _____ number of parents.
9. Managers have so far refused to _____ or deny reports that up to 200 jobs are to go.
10. How much discount do I get if I order this _____?

Task 6: Translate the following sentences into Chinese.

1. While the transaction service platform builds a platform business mode that can realize the online trading and payment for both the supply and purchasing parties.
2. The open platforms achieve the systematic docking of applications and platforms, and build an ecosystem itself based on the platform.
3. Under this mode, Cross-border E-commerce enterprises purchase products in bulk from overseas and the products are shipped and stored in the domestic bonded areas.
4. Under this mode, after consumers place orders in Cross-border E-commerce platforms, E-commerce enterprises or declaration enterprises declare through the Cross-border E-commerce system.
5. For express customs clearance model, after the orders are confirmed, the overseas suppliers directly mail the goods to the consumers from abroad through international express delivery without the customs documents.

Part D　The Status Quo and Development Trend of Cross-border E-commerce

1. The Status Quo of Cross-border E-commerce

Currently, the Cross-border E-commerce is growing at a fast speed. There are various factors which have contributed to this phenomenon. First, the rapid development of Internet as well as mature and advanced technologies has laid a solid foundation for it. Second, it has enjoyed a favorable policy support from the government. Third, the changes in consumer needs have also catalyzed the development of Cross-border E-commerce. More consumers need to purchase goods unavailable in their home countries and wish to buy authentic products directly from foreign countries. Fourth, successful platforms have set a good example and provided a rich experience for those who want to join the Cross-border E-commerce market. Finally, the COVID 19 epidemic has a profound influence on the consumers' consumption habits and behavior, which has greatly promoted the development of global E-commerce, and created new opportunities and challenges for Cross-border E-commerce. Although, it has been developing at a high speed, it still faces some dilemmas and problems like limited supply channels, logistics restrictions, online payment, after-sales service problems, fake products as well as non-standard or illegal operations.

2. The Development Trend of Cross-border E-commerce

Based on the fast-growing Cross-border E-commerce and its current problems and challenges, the future of Cross-border E-commerce will be more mature, aiming at reducing economic cost, facilitating global trade and promoting the long-term steady economic development. First, the increasingly fierce competition urges the businesses to reposition their products and optimize their platforms to make them more consumer-friendly. Second, laws and policies related to Cross-border E-commerce will be carried out to standardize the security of goods, taxes, logistics, etc. The uneven situation of Cross-border E-commerce will be improved to provide regulations and rules for businesses, which will promote the orderly market competition, protect the legitimate rights and interests of consumers and drive purchasing and the further development of Cross-border E-commerce.

Questions

1. What are the factors leading to the popularity of Cross-border E-commerce?
2. What are the challenges and possible solutions for the Cross-border E-commerce enterprises?

New Words and Terms

1. favorable	adj. 有利的
2. catalyze	v. 催化
3. epidemic	n. 疫情
4. dilemma	n. 困境
5. urge	v. 催促；鞭策
6. reposition	v. 重新定位
7. optimize	v. 优化
8. standardize	v. 标准化
9. uneven	adj. 不均衡的
10. security	n. 安全性
11. regulation	n. 条例
12. orderly	adj. 有序的
13. legitimate	adj. 合法的
14. lay a solid foundation for	奠定坚实的基础
15. have a profound influence on	对…有深远影响

Exercises

Task 7：Complete the following sentences with the words or phrases in the box.

mature	favorable	uneven	dilemma
orderly	legitimate	regulation	optimize

1. There exists an _____ distribution of resources.
2. There seems to be so many rules and _____ these days.
3. They need to _____ the use of available resources.
4. The response has been overwhelmingly _____.
5. Most scientists believe it is _____ to use animals in medical research.
6. We are _____ enough to disagree on this issue but still respect each other.
7. I'm in a _____ about this job offer.
8. She needs to organize her ideas in a more _____ way.

Task 8：Translate the following sentences into Chinese.

1. More consumers need to purchase goods unavailable in their home countries and wish

to buy authentic products directly from foreign countries.
2. Finally, the COVID 19 epidemic has a profound influence on the consumers' consumption habits and behavior, which has greatly promoted the development of global E-commerce, and created new opportunities and challenges for Cross-border E-commerce.
3. First, the increasingly fierce competition urges the businesses to reposition their products and optimize their platforms to make them more consumer-friendly.
4. Laws and policies related to Cross-border E-commerce will be carried out to standardize the security of goods, taxes, logistics, etc.
5. The uneven situation of Cross-border E-commerce will be improved to provide regulations and rules for businesses, which will promote the orderly market competition, protect the legitimate rights and interests of consumers.

Learning Aims Achievement and Test

Section	Overview of Cross-border E-commerce		Class hours		course credit	
Level	Medium	Capability	Be able to identify the different classifications of Cross-border E-commerce and the different models of Export and Import Cross-border E-commerce		subtask	4
Number	Contents		Criteria			Score
1	basic concept		Be able to tell what is Cross-border E-commerce and its significance.			
2	Cross-border E-commerce classifications		Be able to tell the ways to classify Cross-border E-commerce and identify each classification			
3	different models of Cross-border E-commerce		Be able to identify the different models of export and import Cross-border E-commerce			
4	the status quo and development trend of Cross-border E-commerce		Be able to tell the factors that contribute to the development of Cross-border E-commerce and list the dilemmas and the future development trend of Cross-border E-commerce			

续表

	Score(1 point for each section)	
Test and Comments	Tutor comments：	

Task Fulfillment Report

Title	
Class	Name	student ID
Task Fulfillment Report			

1. Present your task and your plan for it.
2. Present the difficulties you came across on completing the task and your solutions.
3. Present what you have learnt through all this process.

Write a report with no less than 200 words.

Scoring Criteria(10-score range)		
Tutor comments：	Attitude	
	Task Amount	
Scoring Rules		

1. Timely finish all tasks.
2. Finish the tasks in reasonable way.
3. Reliable, coherent, logical and intelligible report.
4. Unfinished task will lead to 1 point deduction, and copy to 5 points deduction.

Keys

Text A

Task 1:
1. enterprise 2. stimulated 3. tremendously 4. authentic 5. shipping 6. multilateral 7. Access 8. intermediary 9. transformation 10. be associated with

Task 2:
1. 如今,来自全世界的消费者都能够从其他国家的网络平台上购买到本国没有或者极其昂贵的产品或服务。

2. 作为促进经济一体化和贸易全球化的技术基础,跨境电商具有战略意义。

3. 对于国家而言,跨境电商作为一种不断发展的全球外贸模式,也能促进国家开放经济的转型和升级,并通过为国家提供新贸易模式的处理方法而建立新的经济增长点。

4. 通过打破渠道垄断、减少中间商、节省交易成本和缩短交易时长,跨境电商能够为企业提供建立品牌和提升消费者品牌意识的有效方法。

5. 他们甚至能够通过跨境电商平台直接从国外便捷地购买产品,以满足其不同的需求。

Text B

Task 3:
1. published 2. browse 3. classified 4. retail 5. settlement 6. third party

Task 4:
1. 跨境B2C(企业对消费者)是指消费者通过电子商务平台直接从不同关境的企业购买产品或服务的国际商业活动。

2. 这种国际活动包括交易达成、通过电子商务平台完成支付和结算、跨境物流产品运输和交易完成。

3. 在下单和完成支付之后,商品由国内卖家发给物流进行运输。

4. 进口跨境电商指的是国内消费者浏览国外卖家的购物平台并进行商品挑选的活动。

5. 一些跨境卖家直接和第三方平台合作,第三方平台将负责物流、清关和商品检验等。

Text C

Task 5:
1. supervision 2. supplier 3. taxation 4. representative 5. sorted 6. distributed 7. premium 8. substantial 9. confirm 10. in bulk

Task 6:
1. 交易服务平台建立了一种能够为供应方和购买方提供线上贸易和支付的平台商业

模式。

　　2. 开放平台实现了应用和平台的系统对接,并建立了一种基于平台本身的生态系统。

　　3. 在这种模式下,跨境电商企业从海外大批量购买产品,其所购买的产品被运输并储存至国内保税仓库区。

　　4. 在这种模式下,当消费者在跨境电商平台下单之后,电子商务企业或申报企业会通过跨境电商系统进行申报。

　　5. 对于快件通关模式,在确定订单之后,海外供应商直接通过国际快递运输将商品从国外邮寄给消费者,而不需要海关单据。

Text D

Task 7：
1. uneven　2. regulations　3. optimize　4. favorable
5. legitimate　6. mature　7. dilemma　8. orderly

Task 8：
1. 更多的消费者需要购买国内没有的商品,并希望直接从国外购买地道的产品。

2. 最后,"新冠"疫情对于消费者的消费习惯和行为产生了深远的影响,这也极大地促进了全球电子商务的发展,并为跨境电商创造了新的机遇和挑战。

3. 首先,越来越激烈的竞争促使企业重新定位它们的产品、优化它们的平台,使其更加符合消费者的需求。

4. 跨境电商的相关法律和政策将会被实施,以此规范产品安全、税收和物流等。

5. 跨境电商的不均衡发展将会得到改善,以此为企业提供法规条例,这些行为将会促进有序的市场竞争,保护消费者的合法权益。

Unit 2
Main Cross-border E-commerce Platforms

Introduction

The fast-growing Cross-border E-commerce has given birth to a large number of Cross-border E-commerce platforms. The top three Cross-border E-commerce platforms are Amazon, AliExpress and eBay. The other popular Cross-border E-commerce platforms include Alibaba, Wish, Shopee, Lazada, Mercado Libre, and so forth. This unit is divided into four parts. The first part introduces two of the top three Cross-border E-commerce platforms Amazon and eBay. The second part focuses on Alibaba and AliExpress. The third part is about Wish. The last part is about Shopee, Lazada and other regional Cross-border E-commerce platforms.

Contents

Part A   Amazon and eBay
Part B   Alibaba and AliExpress
Part C   Wish
Part D   Shopee, Lazada and Other Regional Cross-border E-commerce Platforms

Learning Aims

- Acquire the basic knowledge about Amazon and eBay.
- Acquire the basic knowledge about Alibaba and AliExpress and the differences between them.
- Acquire the basic knowledge about Wish.
- Acquire the basic knowledge about Shopee, Lazada and other regional Cross-border E-commerce platforms.
- Learn words, phrases, expressions and terms in this unit about the main Cross-border E-commerce platforms.

Capability Aims

- Be able to talk in English about the basic information covered in this unit

concerning the main Cross-border E-commerce platforms.
- Be able to identify each Cross-border E-commerce platform and their respective features and businesses.
- Be able to analyze each platform's pros and cons and choose a suitable Cross-border E-commerce platform based on personal needs.

Related Materials

Part A   Amazon and eBay

1. Amazon

picture 2-1

Amazon, based in Seattle, Washington State, is the largest network E-commerce <u>corporation</u> in the United States. It is one of the earliest companies to start <u>running</u> E-commerce on the Internet. Founded in 1994, with the only business of selling books on its website, it has now widened its businesses to other services, such as electronics, <u>domestic appliances</u>, food, toys, jewelry and so forth. It has become the world's second-largest Internet enterprise and the online <u>retailer</u> with the widest variety of products <u>around the whole globe</u>. The goal of Amazon is to become the world's most <u>customer-centered</u> enterprise with separate retail websites for the United States, the United Kingdom, France, Canada, Germany <u>and so forth</u>.

Amazon is one of the most visited websites in the world with its easy-to-use <u>interface</u> and high number of sellers. The flow of Amazon, which supports the whole world, is a magic <u>existence</u>. The flow of Amazon is equal to five ones of AliExpress or eBay. Amazon <u>takes up</u> about half of all the sales of Cross-border E-commerce. <u>Under the leadership of</u> **Jeff Bezos**, Amazon <u>ranks</u> the first among all the Cross-border E-commerce enterprises within a few years. In 2020, during the epidemic, Jeff Bezos became the wealthiest person around the whole globe <u>owing to</u> Amazon. Someone jokingly comments that Cross-border E-commerce is divided into two types, one is Amazon, and the other is "other platforms".

In terms of business models, Amazon is divided into Amazon B2C and Amazon B2B. Amazon is <u>deemed</u> as a typical B2C E-commerce company, which facilitates B2C selling. It <u>serves as</u> a <u>medium</u> and platform for businesses and consumers. It <u>profits</u> from directly selling to consumers books, electronics and daily necessities such as milk, cereal, sofa and so forth online at reasonable prices. With its widened products, reasonable prices and mature logistics, it has greatly attracted consumers, maintained the consumer base and improved competitiveness. While Amazon B2B (Amazon Business) is a new business model launched by Amazon for enterprise clients, selling machines, office supplies and other products. As a new business model, Amazon hopes it can improve the relationship between Amazon and those sellers who only do business with companies by providing the Amazon platform with a large variety of products. The feature of Amazon B2B is that the products are sold directly by Amazon platform or sellers through a third-party platform. And Amazon charges the third-party sellers a commission and the commission varies from products to products.

2. eBay

picture 2-2

eBay was founded by Pierre Omidyar in 1995 in the name of Auctionweb in San Jose, California, the United States. In 1997, eBay was officially used in place of Auctionweb. It is an online auction and shopping website which allows consumers and businesses around the whole globe to buy and sell a broad variety of goods and services online. Now, eBay has more than 147 million registered users, and sellers from about 30 countries. With more than millions of products sold every day, eBay has become the world's largest e-marketplace. And it has also become a multinational E-commerce corporation, which facilitates both online B2B and C2C sales, making it one of the top three Cross-border E-commerce platforms.

Originally, eBay started its business as an auction website, which was built by its founder Omidyar to help his girlfriend to communicate with all the fans of Pez candy boxes in the United States. But soon, the website was full of fans collecting Pez candy boxes, Barbie dolls and other products, which leads eBay to gradually become a great success of online auction. Now, it has expanded its original auction business to other services, such as online shopping covering a wide variety of goods. And it also has separate websites for the United Kingdom, Australia, China, Canada, Germany and many other countries.

eBay mainly profits from charging each auction and each successful auction commissions as well as its subsidiary company **PayPal** (an online payment service provider) and online shopping. eBay and PayPal are like our domestic **Taobao** and **Alipay**. The former is for opening a store and the latter is for payment. But in 2018, eBay ended its long-time cooperation with PayPal and began to cooperate with Apple and **Square**.

Questions

1. What is Amazon?
2. What are the two business models of Amazon?
3. What is eBay?
4. What's the relationship between eBay and PayPal?

Notes

1. Jeff Bezos：杰夫•贝索斯，创办了全球最大的网上书店亚马逊，于 1999 年当选《时代》周刊年度人物。
2. PayPal：于 1988 年建立，是总部设在美国加利福尼亚州圣荷塞的在线支付服务商，致力于提供普惠金融服务，通过技术创新与战略合作为资金管理和移动创造更好的方式，为转账、付款或收款提供灵活选择，帮助个人及企业参与全球经济；2002 年在纳斯达克上市，随后被 eBay 收购；2018 年，eBay 终止了其与 PayPal 的长期合作伙伴关系。
3. Alipay：支付宝(中国)网络技术有限公司，是国内的第三方支付平台，成立于 2004 年，致力于为企业和个人提供简单、安全、快速、便捷的支付解决方案，旗下有"支付宝"和"支付宝钱包"两个独立品牌；自 2014 年第二季度开始成为全球最大的移动支付厂商。
4. Taobao：淘宝网，是亚太地区较大的网络零售商圈，由阿里巴巴集团在 2003 年创立，是深受国人欢迎的网购零售平台；随着淘宝网规模的扩大和用户数量的增加，其也从单一的 C2C 网络集市变成包括 C2C、团购、分销、拍卖等多种电子商务模式的综合性零售商圈，目前已成为世界范围的电子商务交易平台之一。
5. Square：是美国的一家移动支付公司，用户利用 Square 提供的移动读卡器配合智能手机使用，可以在任何网络状态下通过应用程序匹配刷卡消费，使消费者、商家可以在任何地方进行付款和收款，并保存相应的消费信息，从而大幅降低了刷卡消费的技术门槛和硬件需求。

New Words and Terms

1. corporation	n. 大型公司
2. run	v. 经营
3. retailer	n. 零售商
4. customer-centered	adj. 消费者为中心的
5. interface	n. 界面

续表

6. existence	n. 存在
7. rank	v. 排列,排名
8. deem	v. 认为
9. medium	n. 媒介
10. profit	v. 盈利
11. necessity	n. 必需品
12. cereal	n. 谷物
13. maintain	v. 维持
14. client	n. 客户
15. charge	v. 收费
16. commission	n. 佣金
17. vary	v. 变化
18. officially	adv. 官方地;正式地
19. auction	n. 拍卖
20. register	v. 注册
21. originally	adv. 最初
22. gradually	adv. 逐渐地
23. subsidiary	adj./n. 附属的;子公司
24. domestic appliance	家居
25. around the whole globe	全球,全世界
26. and so forth	等等
27. take up	占据
28. under the leadership of	在…的领导下
29. owing to	由于
30. serve as	充当…角色;用作
31. consumer base	客户群

Exercises

Task 1: Complete the following sentences with the words or phrases in the box.

interface	rank	deem	medium	charge
commission	vary	register	subsidiary	serve as

Unit 2　Main Cross-border E-commerce Platforms

1. You must bring your insurance card with you when you _____ with a dentist or doctor.
2. We won't _____ for delivery if you pay now.
3. It features an easy-to-use dynamic _____ for drawing and analyzing sophisticated geometric structures.
4. Her death should _____ a warning to other young people.
5. They _____ that he was no longer capable of managing the business.
6. The dealer takes a 20% _____ on the sales he makes.
7. Advertising is a powerful _____ .
8. The company is mainly responsible for the procurement and delivery of production materials needed by the Group and its _____ branches.
9. He _____ high among the pioneers of 20th century chemical technology.
10. Medical treatment _____ greatly from state to state.

Task 2: Translate the following sentences into Chinese.

1. Founded in 1994, with the only business of selling books on its website, it has now widened its businesses to other services, such as electronics, domestic appliances, food, toys, jewelry and so forth.
2. With its widened products, reasonable prices and mature logistics, it has greatly attracted consumers, maintained the consumer base and improved competitiveness.
3. As a new business model, Amazon hopes it can improve the relationship between Amazon and those sellers who only do business with companies by providing the Amazon platform with a large variety of products.
4. It is an online auction and shopping website which allows consumers and businesses around the whole globe to buy and sell a broad variety of goods and services online.
5. eBay mainly profits from charging each auction and each successful auction commissions as well as its subsidiary company PayPal (an online payment service provider) and online shopping.

Part B   Alibaba and AliExpress

1. Alibaba

Alibaba Group was co-founded by Jack Ma and 17 other founders in 1999 in Hangzhou, Zhejiang, China. It is Asia's leading E-commerce conglomerate which offers an array of different online services including B2B, B2C and C2C online shopping platforms. The mission of the Group is to make it easy to do business anywhere and anytime by equipping suppliers with necessary tools to reach a global audience for their products and by helping buyers find products and supplies quickly and efficiently. The

picture 2-3

main business of Alibaba Group involve E-commerce, online payment, B2B online transaction market, **cloud computing**, logistics and so on. The major platforms of Alibaba Group include Alibaba.com, AliExpress, Tmall and Taobao. Alibaba.com is Asia's leading B2B online marketplace which facilitates global wholesale trade. It provides hundreds of millions of goods in more than 40 different categories including electronics, machinery, apparels and so forth. From this platform, global small and medium-sized enterprises, located in over 200 countries and regions, can purchase goods at wholesale prices, making a profit by reselling those goods in their domestic markets. While the sellers can list their products on this platform for free but can also pay for further benefits like greater exposure on the platform or unlimited product listings. Tmall is a B2C online marketplace which focuses on branded products. It integrates thousands of brands and manufacturers to provide one-stop services for businesses and consumers. It also provides premium services like 100% quality assurance products, 7-day return, and so forth. In 2014, Tmall Global was officially launched by Alibaba Group, which directly supplies domestic consumers with overseas original imported products. Taobao is a C2C online marketplace where small and individual sellers can directly list products on the platforms for the consumers to browse. Founded in 2003 by Alibaba Group, it is a relatively large online retailer and central business platform in the Asian-Pacific region. With the expanding of its scale and the growth of its users, it has changed from a single C2C online marketplace to a comprehensive retailing business platform that includes C2C, group buying, distributing, auction and other E-commerce modes. It has now become one of the world-wide E-commerce transaction platforms. AliExpress is to be introduced in detail in the next part.

2. AliExpress

As mentioned above, AliExpress is one of the major platforms of Alibaba Group. It is a Cross-border E-commerce platform founded by Alibaba Group in 2010 in Hangzhou,

AliExpress

picture 2-4

Zhejiang, China to <u>target at</u> international market. Widely known as "International Taobao", it targets at overseas buyers and clients from over 220 countries and regions. Those international buyers and clients are able to purchase directly from the manufacturers and distributors mainly based in China through this global B2C marketplace. Its top consumer markets are Russia, the United States, the United Kingdom, Spain, France, Canada, Australia, Israel, Brazil and so forth. In May 2017, Alibaba Group announced that all **B&R** countries and regions were covered on this platform, whose total users have <u>accounted for</u> more than 45% of all AliExpress users. And the top five B&R countries in <u>purchasing power</u> are Russia, Ukraine, Israel, Belarus and Poland.

As the world's third-largest English online shopping website and one of the world's top three Cross-border E-commerce platforms, AliExpress makes <u>secured transactions</u> through Alipay Account as well as ships and delivers through international logistics channels. 30 <u>primary categories</u> with more than 6000 products are sold on AliExpress platform such as 3C, costumes, domestic appliances, <u>accessories</u> and so forth. Its major businesses include apparel and fashion, mobile phones and <u>communications</u>, shoes and bags, beauty and health, jewelry and watches and so forth.

Serving as the only global online trading platform of Alibaba Group, AliExpress has its own advantages like reasonable platform entrance fee compared with other platforms and one-stop translation of products, products releasing, payment, logistics and other services.

Questions

1. What are the world's top three Cross-border E-commerce platforms?
2. What is Alibaba Group and its mission?
3. What are the four major platforms of Alibaba Group?
4. What is AliExpress?

Notes

1. cloud computing：云计算，"云"实际上就是一个网络，狭义来讲，云计算就是一种提供资源的网络，使用者可以随时获取"云"上的资源，按需求量使用，并且可以看成是无限扩展的，只要按使用量付费即可；广义来讲，云计算是与信息技术、软件、互联网相关的一种服务，这种计算资源共享池叫作"云"，云计算把许多计算资源集合起来，通过软件实现自动化管理，只需要很少人的参与，就能快速提供资源；云计算的核心概念是以互联网为中心,在网站上提供快速且安全的云计算服务与数据存储服务,让每一个使用互联网的人都可以使用网络上庞大的资源。

2. B&R:"一带一路"(The Belt and Road),是"丝绸之路经济带"和"21世纪海上丝绸之路"的简称,是于2013年由中国提出的合作倡议。"一带一路"旨在借用古代"丝绸之路"的历史符号,高举和平发展的旗帜,积极发展与沿线国家的经济合作伙伴关系,共同打造政治互信、经济融合、文化包容的利益共同体、命运共同体和责任共同体。

3. 3C:3C产品,是指计算机类、通信类和消费类电子产品的统称,亦称信息家电,例如电脑、平板电脑、手机或数字音频播放器等,其发展基础是集成电路与互联网的快速发展。

New Words and Terms

1.	conglomerate	n. 企业集团
2.	mission	n. 使命
3.	wholesale	adj./n. 批发的;批发
4.	machinery	n. 机械装置;机器
5.	apparel	n. 服装;服饰
6.	exposure	n. 曝光
7.	branded	adj. 名牌的
8.	integrate	v. 整合;融合
9.	scale	n. 规模
10.	comprehensive	adj. 综合的
11.	distribute	v. 分销
12.	accessory	n. 饰品
13.	communication	n. 通信;通讯
14.	an array of	大量的
15.	equip...with	使…具有;配备有…
16.	product listing	产品详情页
17.	quality assurance	质量保证
18.	group buying	团购
19.	target at	目标指向
20.	account for	占据
21.	purchasing power	购买力
22.	secured transaction	担保交易
23.	primary category	一级类目

Exercises

Task 3: Complete the following sentences with the words or phrases in the box.

| conglomerate | wholesale | integrate | comprehensive | distribute |
| scale | account for | equip...with | an array of | target at |

1. They spent a lot of money _____ the school _____ new computers.
2. Transport planning should be _____ with energy policy.
3. Travel Ventures International is a leading multinational _____ headquartered in London, the United Kingdom.
4. Large firms benefit from economies of _____.
5. We offer our customers a _____ range of financial products.
6. Afro-Americans _____ 12% of the US population.
7. Jade has always been a _____ business as the main item.
8. The programme is _____ improving the health of women of all ages.
9. Milk is _____ to the local shops by Herald's Dairies.
10. There was a vast _____ colors to choose from.

Task 4: Translate the following sentences into Chinese.

1. The mission of the Group is to make it easy to do business anywhere and anytime by equipping suppliers with necessary tools to reach a global audience for their products and by helping buyers find products and supplies quickly and efficiently.
2. From this platform, global small and medium-sized enterprises, locating in over 200 countries and regions, can purchase goods at wholesale prices, making a profit by reselling those goods in their domestic markets.
3. With the expanding of its scale and the growth of its users, it has changed from a single C2C online marketplace to a comprehensive retailing business platform that includes C2C, group buying, distributing, auction and other E-commerce modes.
4. As the world's third-largest English online shopping website and one of the world's top three Cross-border E-commerce platforms, AliExpress makes secured transactions through Alipay Account as well as ships and delivers through international logistics channels.
5. Serving as the only global online trading platform of Alibaba Group, AliExpress has its own advantages like reasonable platform entrance fee compared with other platforms and one-stop translation of products, products releasing, payment, logistics and other services.

Picture 2-5

Part C Wish

Wish was founded in 2011 by two engineers Peter Szulczewski from **Google** and Danny Zhang from **Yahoo** in Silicon Valley, the United States. About 90% sellers on this platform are from China. It is a mobile shopping APP, which supports Android, iOS and web. In 2013, Wish successfully transformed into Cross-border E-commerce. It is the largest mobile E-commerce platform in North America and Europe as well as the world's six largest E-commerce platform. Wish advocates to provide consumers with premium products at reasonable prices. As a simplified platform, Wish is devoted to making it easier for traders to sell and the buyers to purchase. Its top consumer markets are mainly the countries and regions located in North America, with a centralized consumer base, enabling the sellers to precisely market for consumers after they enter the Wish platform.

Different from the world's top three Cross-border E-commerce platforms which operate on PC terminals, Wish is the first platform mainly operating on mobile terminals. With the development of smart phones, the ways and scenes that people use Internet has undergone great changes. It has become faster for people to obtain information with their shortened reading time and fragmented information reading. And Wish has come into being by grasping this opportunity. Through following the consumption trend through mobile terminals, the interfaces of this APP vary from mobile terminal to mobile terminal with the same user seeing different interfaces at different times. Because it features the mobile terminal, it is accessible to consumers anytime and anywhere and almost all the orders are placed and completed through mobile phones. Meanwhile, based on the precise **recommendation algorithm** technology, this APP is able to send related product information to users based on the users' preferences, habits, browsing records and shopping records. While the users can also set the platform to only browse the preferred products according to their own habits and preferences.

    Although Wish has a short history, it develops at a fast speed with its own <u>distinctive characteristics</u>.

Questions

1. What is Wish?
2. What is the biggest difference between Wish and the world's top three Cross-border E-commerce platforms?
3. What are the characteristics of Wish?

Notes

1. Google：谷歌公司，成立于 1998 年，被公认为全球规模最大的搜索引擎公司，是一家位于美国的跨国科技企业，业务范围包括互联网搜索、云计算、广告技术等，同时开发并提供了大量基于互联网的产品与服务，其利润主要来自于 AdWords 等广告服务。
2. Yahoo：雅虎，是美国著名的互联网门户网站，总部设在美国加利福尼亚州圣克拉克市，其服务范围包括搜索引擎、电子邮件、新闻等，业务遍及 24 个国家和地区，为全球超过 5 亿的独立用户提供多元化的网络服务；同时也是一家全球性的互联网通信、商贸及媒体公司，是全球第一家提供互联网导航服务的公司。
3. recommendation algorithm：推荐算法，是计算机领域中的一种算法，它通过一些数学算法推测出用户可能喜欢的东西，目前应用较多的地方主要是网络；个性化推荐概念的首次出现是在 1995 年举办的美国人工智能协会上。

New Words and Terms

1. mobile	adj. 移动的
2. advocate	v. 提倡；倡导
3. simplified	adj. 简化的
4. trader	n. 商人
5. centralized	adj. 集中的
6. precisely	adv. 精确地
7. market	v. 营销
8. operate	v. 操作
9. terminal	n. 终端
10. scene	n. 场景
11. grasp	v. 抓住
12. trend	n. 趋势
13. accessible	adj. 可到达的；可接近的；可进入的

		续表
14. preference	n. 偏爱	
15. distinctive	adj. 与众不同的	
16. characteristic	n. 特征	
17. be devoted to	致力于	
18. locate in	坐落于	
19. come into being	产生；形成	

Exercises

Task 5: Complete the following sentences with the words or phrases in the box.

trader	precisely	market	terminal
accessible	preference	come into being	distinctive

1. If you could ever figure out how to _____ this you'd make a fortune.
2. Computers should be made readily _____ to teachers and pupils.
3. Wish is operated on mobile _____ .
4. Many elderly people expressed a strong _____ to live in their own homes.
5. To the surprise of many Wall Street _____, the dollars rose yesterday.
6. Early in its history, the company recognized the need for a _____ package to sell its product.
7. It is difficult to know _____ how much impact the changes will leave.
8. The issue of guaranteeing the consumers' right and interest does not _____ until the human history developed into a certain stage.

Task 6: Translate the following sentences into Chinese.

1. Its top consumer markets are mainly the countries and regions located in North America, with a centralized consumer base, enabling the sellers to precisely market for consumers after they enter the Wish platform.
2. Different from the world's top three Cross-border E-commerce platforms which operate on PC terminals, Wish is the first platform mainly operating on mobile terminals.
3. It has become faster for people to obtain information with their shortened reading time and fragmented information reading.
4. Through following the consumption trend through mobile terminals, the interfaces of this APP vary from mobile terminal to mobile terminal with the same user seeing different interfaces at different times.

5. Meanwhile, based on the precise recommendation algorithm technology, this APP is able to send related product information to users based on the users' preferences, habits, browsing records and shopping records.

Part D Shopee, Lazada and Other Regional Cross-border E-commerce Platforms

1. Shopee and Lazada

picture 2-6

Shopee, a subsidiary of **Sea Group**, was founded and headquartered in Singapore in 2015. It is a Southeast Asian E-commerce platform that grows at the fastest speed. Having started in Singapore, it later expands its businesses to Malaysia, Thailand, Indonesia, Vietnam, the Philippines, Taiwan, China and so forth. It possesses a wide range of products including consumer electronics, domestic appliances, beauty and health, mother and baby products, apparel and fashion, fitness equipment and so forth.

In 2016, Shopee set up offices in Shen Zhen and Hong Kong, China to comprehensively begin developing its Cross-border businesses with China. It has even built a one-stop Cross-border solution for Chinese Cross-border sellers by providing with them logistics, language, payment, **ERP** and so forth. Currently, the seven major markets of Shopee are all open to Chinese Cross-border sellers.

Since its founding, Cross-border business has always been the engine for Shopee to achieve its rapid development. Cross-border business also serves as an important support for Shopee's core competitiveness. Being confident about its Cross-border business, Shopee has been continuously increasing the investment of strategic resources.

Lazada, headquartered in Singapore, was founded in 2012. It is the largest E-commerce platform in Southeast Asia. Lazada can be considered as the Southeast Asian version of Amazon or **JD.com**. Its target users are mainly based in Indonesia, Malaysia, the Philippines, Thailand and so forth. It primarily sells 3C products.

It first introduces **Double** 11 into Southeast Asia. In 2016, responding to the strategic goals of the globalization of Alibaba, Lazada accepted the investment of Alibaba, which made Alibaba its **holding company**. And starting from then, Lazada has become a flagship E-commerce platform of Alibaba Group in Southeast Asia.

Lazada has built its own logistics network by taking advantage of the platform's port-to-port logistics capability and full control over supply chains. Now, it has over 30 warehouse centers in 17 Southeast Asian cities. It has also built in each country self-operated warehouses, sorting centers, electronic science and technology facilities, networks matching its cooperation partners, Cross-border and the "last kilometer" logistics capability. Under the support of technology, Lazada is devoted to redefining retail experience, tracking the changes of consumer demands in the first place through real-time data. In particular, Lazada provides after-sales services like 1-year warranty, freight free and 14-day unconditional return or exchange.

Shopee is comparatively more popular in China, but the market share of Shopee is less than that of the Lazada. The main reason is that Shopee massively attracts investment in China, with offline exhibitions and online investment fairs. While the investment activities of Lazada are less exposed to people, it mainly focuses on platform optimization, financial payment and the support of local store sellers without trying to attract investment massively. If Lazada wants to attract investment, it will be easier than Shopee because it has embedded a Lazada port in every Alibaba platform. Previously, AliExpress became popular by this way.

2. Other Regional Cross-border E-commerce platforms

Picture 2-7

Realizing the business opportunities arising from E-commerce, many enterprises are trying to transform from traditional foreign trade to Cross-border E-commerce. Under this context, many regional Cross-border E-commerce platforms emerge in different countries. In this part, several regional Cross-border E-commerce platforms will be briefly introduced.

DHgate, founded in 2004 by Wang Shutong, is a leading Chinese B2B Cross-border E-commerce transaction platform. It is also China's first platform to devote itself to helping small and medium-sized enterprises to step into the international market. It has developed a <u>brand-new</u> international trade by integrating traditional international trade with E-commerce. And it has built a one-stop solution for online international trade by providing various related services. It aims at building an "online silk road" to make online transaction become easier, safer and more efficient. It adopts the commission system, only charges after successful transactions among the sellers and buyers.

Mercado Libre, founded in 1999, is the leading E-commerce platform in Latin America. It is headquartered in Buenos Aires, Argentina. Currently, its E-commerce businesses mainly cover 18 Latin American countries like Brazil, Argentina, Mexico, Chile and Columbia. It provides millions of users with a wide range of products and services such as domestic appliances, technology, cars, sports and outdoor, books, toys and baby products, fashion, and so forth. It aims at bringing E-commerce to everyone and everywhere. To achieve this goal, it provides its own transport and payment services.

Flipkart was founded in 2007 by two previous Amazon staffs. After its founding, it rapidly becomes the leading E-commerce retailer platform in India. The patterns of this platform are extremely similar to those of Amazon. It also started its business by selling books online. Now it has expanded its businesses to other products. It teaches Indians to shop online and builds a <u>cash-on-delivery</u> system to better serve the Indians. In 2018, it was <u>acquired</u> by Walmart.

Cdiscount, founded in 1998, is the leading local E-commerce platform in France. It is headquartered in Bordeaux, France, subsidiary to Casino Group. The products sold on this platform are 3C electronics, domestic appliances, gardening, outdoors, recreation, infant or baby products, bags, suitcases, toys and other daily necessities. It supports **FBM** and the use of the platform's own overseas warehouses.

Questions

1. What is Lazada?
2. What are the advantages of Lazada?
3. What is Shopee?
4. What is the engine and core competitiveness of Shopee?
5. How much do you know about other regional Cross-border E-commerce platforms?

Notes

1. Sea Group:是目前东南亚地区估值最高的集游戏、电商、数字支付业务于一体的电子商务初创公司,由华人企业家 Forrest Li 于 2009 年在新加坡成立,主要业务包括在线游戏平台 Garena、电商平台 Shopee 以及数字支付服务 AirPay;公司使命是利用技术为东南亚消费者和小微企业创造更美好的生活;腾讯是其第一大股东。

2. ERP:Enterprise Resource Planning,企业资源计划,是指建立在信息技术基础上,集信息技术与先进管理思想于一体,以系统化的管理思想为企业员工及决策层提供决策手段的管理平台;其核心思想是供应链管理,它对于改善企业业务流程、提高企业核心竞争力具有显著作用。

3. JD.com:京东,中国自营式电商企业,于 1998 年由刘强东在北京中关村创立,旗下设有京东商城、京东金融、拍拍网、京东智能等,2014 年在美国纳斯达克证券交易所正式挂牌上市。

4. Double 11:"双十一"购物狂欢节,源于淘宝商城(天猫)在 2009 年举办的网络促销活动;"双十一"成为了中国电子商务行业的年度盛事,并且逐渐影响到国际电子商务行业,其实质是网络促销。

5. holding company:是指通过持有某一公司一定数量的股份,而对该公司进行控制的公司;控股公司按控股方式分为纯粹控股公司和混合控股公司;纯粹控股公司不直接从事生产经营业务,只是凭借其持有的其他公司的股份进行资本运营;混合控股公司除通过控股进行资本运营外,也从事一些生产经营业务。

6. FBM:Fulfillment by Merchant,指由卖家自行发货,又称自发货。

New Words and Terms

1.	possess	v. 拥有
2.	fitness	n. 健身
3.	comprehensively	adv. 全面地
4.	primarily	adv. 主要地
5.	flagship	n. 旗舰
6.	port-to-port	adj. 端对端的
7.	redefine	v. 重新定义
8.	warranty	n. 保修期
9.	massively	adv. 大规模地
10.	offline	adj. 线下的
11.	fair	n. 展销会
12.	embed	v. 嵌入
13.	context	n. 背景
14.	emerge	v. 出现
15.	cash-on-delivery	adj. 货到付款的

续表

16. acquire	v. 收购
17. brand-new	adj. 全新的
18. core competitiveness	核心竞争力
19. target users	目标用户
20. respond to	回应
21. take advantage of	利用
22. sorting center	分拣中心
23. in the first place	第一时间
24. freight free	免运费

Exercises

Task 7: Complete the following sentences with the words or phrases in the box.

| flagship | redefine | warranty | fair | acquire |
| emerge | embed | brand-new | take advantage of | respond to |

1. Don't lend them the car, they're _____ you.

2. The new constitution _____ the powers of the president.

3. The sun _____ from behind the clouds.

4. Many enterprises attended this trade _____.

5. The car is still under _____.

6. _____ the news, Mr. Watt appealed for calm.

7. The firm has just opened a _____ store in Las Vegas.

8. His clothes looked _____.

9. The company has _____ new sites for real estate development.

10. A piece of glass was _____ in her hand.

Task 8: Translate the following sentences into Chinese.

1. It has even built a one-stop Cross-border solution for Chinese Cross-border sellers by providing with them logistics, language, payment, ERP and so forth.

2. In 2016, responding to the strategic goals of the globalization of Alibaba, Lazada accepted the investment of Alibaba, which made Alibaba its holding company.

3. It has also built in each country self-operated warehouses, sorting centers, electronic science and technology facilities, networks matching its cooperation partners, Cross-border and the "last kilometer" logistics capability.

4. It is also China's first platform to devote itself to helping small and medium-sized

enterprises to step into the international market. It has developed a brand-new international trade by integrating traditional international trade with E-commerce.
5. The products sold on this platform are 3C electronics, domestic appliances, gardening, outdoors, recreation, infant or baby products , bags, suitcases, toys and other daily necessities.

Learning Aims Achievement and Test

Section	Main Cross-border E-commerce Platforms		Class hours		course credit	
Level	Medium	Capability	Be able to identify and analyze each Cross-border E-commerce platform and their respective features, businesses, pros and cons		subtask	4
Number	Contents		Criteria			Score
1	basic concept		Be able to talk in English about the basic information covered in this unit concerning the main Cross-border E-commerce platforms			
2	main Cross-border E-commerce platforms		Be able to identify each Cross-border E-commerce platform and their respective features and businesses			
3	Pros and cons of each platform		Be able to analyze each platform's pros and cons			
4	Choose a suitable platform		Be able to choose a suitable Cross-border E-commerce platform based on personal needs			
Test and Comments	Score(1 point for each section)					
	Tutor comments:					

Task Fulfillment Report

Title				
Class		Name		student ID
Task Fulfillment Report					

1. Present your task and your plan for it.
2. Present the difficulties you came across on completing the task and your solutions.
3. Present what you have learnt through all this process.

Write a report with no less than 300 words.

	Scoring Criteria(10-score range)	
Tutor comments:	Attitude	
	Task Amount	
Scoring Rules		

1. Timely finish all tasks.
2. Finish the tasks in reasonable way.
3. Reliable, coherent, logical and intelligible report.
4. Unfinished task will lead to 1 point deduction, and copy to 5 points deduction.

Keys

Text A

Task 1:

1. register 2. charge 3. interface 4. serve as 5. deemed
6. commission 7. medium 8. subsidiary 9. ranked 10. varies

Task 2:

1. 亚马逊成立于1994年,最开始以在网上售卖书籍作为唯一业务;现在,亚马逊已经拓展了其他业务,例如电子产品、家用器械、食物、玩具、珠宝等。

2. 因其拓展的业务、合理的价格和成熟的物流,它极大地吸引了消费者,维护了客户群并提升了竞争力。

3. 作为一种新的商业模式,亚马逊希望能够通过提供各种产品提升自己和那些只与公司做交易的卖家的关系。

4. 它是一个允许全球消费者和企业交易各种线上产品和服务的线上拍卖及购物网站。

5. 易趣主要通过对每笔拍卖和每笔成功的拍卖收取佣金,以及其子公司 PayPal(一家线上支付服务供应商)和线上购物盈利。

Text B

Task 3:

1. equipping...with   2. integrated   3. conglomerate   4. scale   5. comprehensive
6. account for   7. wholesale   8. targeting at   9. distributed   10. array

Task 4:

1. 这个集团的使命是通过为供应商提供各种工具来吸引全球消费者,并帮助买家快速有效地找到产品和供应,使得在任何时间、任何地点做生意都能变得更容易。

2. 来自全球超过 200 个国家和地区的中小企业能够从这个平台以批发价购买产品,然后通过在他们的国内市场售卖这些产品而获取利润。

3. 随着其规模和用户数量的增加,它已经从单纯的 C2C 线上集市变成了一个综合的,包含 C2C、团购、分销、拍卖和其他电子商务模式的零售商业平台。

4. 作为全球第三大英文线上购物网站和全球排名前三的跨境电商平台,速卖通通过支付宝账户以及国际物流渠道的运输和发货来确保安全交易。

5. 作为阿里巴巴集团唯一的全球线上贸易平台,速卖通有着其自身的优势,如较之其他平台更加合理的平台入驻费以及一站式的产品翻译、产品发布、支付、物流和其他服务。

Text C

Task 5:

1. market   2. accessible   3. terminal   4. preference
5. traders   6. distinctive   7. precisely   8. come into being

Task 6:

1. 它领先的消费者市场主要是北美洲的一些国家和地区,这些集中的客户群使得卖家能够在进入 Wish 平台后对消费者进行精准营销。

2. 不同于在 PC 端操作的全球三大跨境电商平台,Wish 是第一个主要在移动端操作的平台。

3. 随着人们阅读时间的变短以及碎片化阅读的普及,人们获取信息的速度也随之变快。

4. 通过移动终端跟踪消费倾向,这款 App 的界面因终端的不同而呈现不同的界面,同一用户在不同时间看到的界面也是不同的。

5. 同时,基于精确的推荐算法技术,这款 App 能够基于用户的喜好、习惯、浏览记录和购物记录向用户推送相关产品的信息。

Text D

Task 7：

1. taking advantage of   2. redefines   3. emerges   4. fair   5. warranty
6. Responding to   7. flagship   8. brand-new   9. acquired   10. embedded

Task 8：

1. 它甚至通过为中国跨境卖家提供物流、语言、支付、ERP 等而为其建立了一站式的跨境解决方案。

2. 2016 年，为响应阿里巴巴全球化的战略目标，Lazada 接受了阿里巴巴集团的投资，从而使阿里巴巴集团成为其控股公司。

3. 它还在每个国家建立了自营仓库、分拣中心、电子科技设备、匹配合作伙伴的网络、跨境和"最后一公里"的物流服务。

4. 它也是中国第一个致力于帮助中小企业踏入国际市场的平台，它通过融合传统国际贸易和电子商务发展出了一种崭新的国际贸易形式。

5. 这个平台上售卖的产品包括 3C、家用器械、园艺、户外、娱乐、婴幼儿产品、包、手提箱、玩具和其他日用必需品。

Unit 3
Opening a Cross-border E-commerce Store

Introduction

This unit is about how to open a Cross-border E-commerce store. It is divided into three parts. The first part is about the preparations for opening a Cross-border E-commerce store. The second part is about registration. In this part, the Cross-border E-commerce platform Wish serves as an example to show detailed procedures and operations about how to register for a store on a Cross-border E-commerce platform. The third part is about launching products on a Cross-border E-commerce platform. This part still takes Wish platform as an example to show how to launch products on a Cross-border E-commerce platform.

Contents

Part A   Preparing for Opening a Cross-border E-commerce Store
Part B   Registering for a Cross-border E-commerce Store
Part C   Launching Products on a Cross-border E-commerce Platform

Learning Aims

- Acquire basic knowledge about the preparations before opening across-border E-commerce store.
- Understand how to register for across-border E-commerce store.
- Understand how to launch products on across-border E-commerce platform.
- Learn words, phrases, expressions and terms in this unit about opening across-border E-commerce store.

Capability Aims

- Be able to talk in English about the basic information covered in this unit concerning opening across-border E-commerce store.
- Be able to register for a Cross-border E-commerce store.

- Be able to launch products on across-border E-commerce platform.

Related Materials

Part A Preparing for Opening a Cross-border E-commerce Store

Preparations for opening a Cross-border E-commerce store is indispensable. They can help deepen the merchants' understanding of Cross-border E-commerce and how to do business on a Cross-border E-commerce platform.

First, the merchants need to choose a type of Cross-border E-commerce based on the different classifications of Cross-border E-commerce.

Second, the merchants should take the market into consideration, whether it targets at America, Europe, Southeast Asia or somewhere else. For example, Amazon, eBay and Wish have the largest market share in Europe and America. AliExpress is most popular in Russia and Spain. Lazada and Shopee are suitable for those who target at Southeast Asia. While for markets in France, Cdiscount or **Fnac** is good choices.

Third, the merchants need to compare and contrast different Cross-border E-commerce platforms such as their respective features, rules, advantages and disadvantages, then choose the most suitable platform. For example, Amazon is the world's top E-commerce transaction platform with large market share and profit while it is demanding in operation and fund. However, regional platforms like Shopee are easier with imperfect platform rules and products SKU.

Fourth, the merchants should have a systematic learning about the chosen Cross-border E-commerce platform, especially about registration, account, the Merchant Terms of Service and some illegal operations to save time and unnecessary cost.

Fifth, the merchants need to prepare required materials to settle in a platform. For Amazon, the required materials include enterprise business license, legal representative ID card, mailbox, mobile phone, VISA credit card. All these information must be true and correct. Otherwise, in the second verification, the store will be banned if you fail to submit required materials. While for Shopee, the required materials only include individual or company business license, legal representative ID card, mobile phone, QQ, mailbox. It is also free to settle in with no second verification, rent or deposit. And the first three months are free of sales commissions.

Sixth, the merchants need to confirm the delivery method, whether it is FBM or delivery by stock up. For Amazon, it has FBM and **FBA**. Shopee has its own logistics channel. You only need to deliver to a transit warehouse of Shopee in a certain country, and Shopee will be responsible for the follow-up distribution, which saves you time and effort.

Seventh, merchants also need to confirm the product category and products based on the market's needs such as religious belief, local customs and practices. For example, Amazon is mainly targeting sellers in Europe and America whose living and income standards are relatively high. Therefore, the products on this platform must have the quality guarantee. Due to the epidemic, the demands for domestic appliances, entertainment products and pet supplies are increasing in these markets. While for Shopee, you are not supposed to sell <u>down coats</u> because of climate situation in Southeast Asia. Meanwhile, you need to integrate all the possible sources of goods to ensure stable supplies.

Finally, the merchants need to build a competitive team. The members in a team need time to cooperate with each other effectively and efficiently to guarantee smooth business operation.

Questions

1. Which platforms are suitable for markets in Europe and America?
2. What are the required materials for registering for a store on Amazon platform?
3. What does FBA and FBM refer to?
4. What are the other possible factors merchants need to take into consideration before opening a Cross-border E-commerce store?

Notes

1. Fnac：法国的一家零售企业，开业于1954年，是法国人购买电子科技产品的首选平台，法国排名第三的文化产品和电器产品零售商，类似京东。
2. FBA：Fulfillment by Amazon, 亚马逊物流服务，成立于2007年，即亚马逊将自身平台开放给第三方卖家，将其库存纳入亚马逊的全球物流网络，为其提供拣货、包装以及终端配送服务，亚马逊则收取服务费用。

New Words and Terms

1. respective	adj. 分别的；各自的
2. demanding	adj. 要求高的；需要高技能的
3. verification	n. 验证
4. deposit	n. 押金
5. down-coat	n. 羽绒服
6. take...into consideration	考虑…
7. merchant terms of services	商家服务条款

续表

8. settle in	入驻
9. legal representative	法定代表人
10. sales commissions	销售佣金
11. transit warehouse	中转仓库

Exercises

Task 1: Complete the following sentences with the words or phrases in the box.

deposit   verification   demanding   respective   take...into consideration

1. Being a salesman is a _____ job.
2. We ask for one month's rent in advance, plus a _____ of $500.
3. We all went back to our _____ homes to wait for news.
4. In this step, the embassy to which he submits the paperwork will choose a service provider, whose job is to process the _____.
5. We will _____ your recent illness _____ when marking your exams.

Task 2: Translate the following sentences into Chinese.

1. Third, the merchants need to compare and contrast different Cross-border E-commerce platforms such as their respective features, rules, advantages and disadvantages, then choose the most suitable platform.
2. Due to the epidemic, the demands for domestic appliances, entertainment products and pet supplies are increasing in these markets.
3. Fourth, the merchants should have a systematic learning about the chosen Cross-border E-commerce platform, especially about registration, account, the Merchant Terms of Service and some illegal operations to save time and unnecessary cost.
4. For Amazon, the required materials include enterprise business license, legal representative ID card, mailbox, mobile phone, VISA credit card.
5. You only need to deliver to a transit warehouse of Shopee in a certain country, and Shopee will be responsible for the follow-up distribution, which saves you time and effort.

Part B Registering for a Cross-border E-commerce Store

This part takes Wish platform as an example to demonstrate the policies for registration and the specific procedures to register for a Cross-border E-commerce Store.

1. Policies for Registration

(1) Information provided at registration must be true and correct. Otherwise, the merchant's account may be at risk of suspension, funds withholding or freeze, user ban, account termination or ban.

(2) Each entity may have one account only. If any company or person has multiple accounts. All accounts risk suspension.

(3) ERP Partners and Private API are subject to Partner Terms of Service. ERP Partners and Private API merchants that are used on Wish are subject to the Wish API Terms of Service.

(4) Merchants must properly safeguard customer data. Failing to properly safeguard personal customer information and data may result in higher penalties, suspension, and/or termination. Examples of improper safeguarding of customer information and data include, but are not limited to:

① Improperly exposing names and addresses of customers to outside parties

② Posting API tokens publicly

③ Sharing passwords to accounts

For more and further registration policies, you can go to the Policy Overview for merchants on Wish platform through this URL: https://merchant.wish.com/policy.

2. Procedures for Registration

Step 1: Open a search engine and input the URL: https://merchant.wish.com/welcome.

Step 2: Enter the homepage, click 'open a store immediately'.

picture 3-1

Step 3: Enter the interface of 'Begin to create your Wish store'. The user can choose to switch the interface language from Chinese to English or to any other language through the top right corner pull-down menu.

picture 3-2

Step 4: Enter the interface of 'set up username'.

picture 3-3

First, the user is required to input e-mail address. This e-mail address will be the user name to log in to the merchant platform in the future.

Second, the user is required to input password. To ensure the user's account security, the password cannot have common combination of digits or letters. Instead, it must have no less than 8 characters which include letters, digits and marks. For example, 'password100@store'.

Third, the user is required to input mobile-phone number and the text in the image on the right side and then click 'send validation code'. If it is successfully sent, a dialog box will appear on the screen like the following picture.

Then, the user is required to click 'OK' and then input the validation code from the mobile phone.

Step 5: At this time, the interface jumps to the 'Merchant Terms of Service'. The

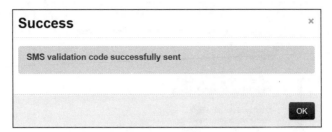

picture 3-4

user is required to read carefully the terms of service and related policies and then click 'I have read and agree to the Merchant Terms of Service'.

picture 3-5

The following picture shows part of the Merchant Terms of Service.

picture 3-6

After all the steps mentioned above have been completed, the user is required to click 'Create Store'.

Step 6: At this time, the interface jumps to 'verification email'. The platform's system has automatically sent the verification email to the user's email address. The user is required to click 'Check my email now'.

The user receives an email and is required to click 'verification mailbox' or the URL in this email.

Step 7: The interface jumps back to 'Wish for Merchants platform'. The user is required to continue filling in information.

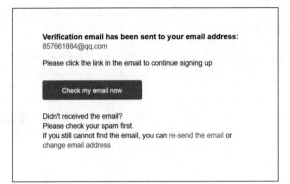

picture 3-7

picture 3-8

picture 3-9

First, the user needs to input a store name. The user cannot use "Wish" in the store name or names that infringe other brands, such as Wish Top One or Nike Store. This platform suggests using a name related to the products like Lucy Jewelry World. And unsuitable names may result in shutdown of the store.

Second, the user needs to input his/her real name, including last name and first name in Chinese. The name must match the certification information in real-name verification.

Third, the user needs to input the office address, including country/region, province/ autonomous region / municipality, city/ county /town, street, house number and zip code and then click 'next' to finish registration.

> ✓ **Congratulations on your successful registration, and please complete the real-name verification as soon as possible.**
>
> Your email is 857661884@qq.com . Please keep this in mind.

picture 3-10

Step 8: Complete the real-name verification so that the user can release products on Wish platform. There are two situations: individual account and company account.

👤 **Real-name verification for individual account**	🏢 **Real-name verification for company account**
① Provide identification information.	① Provide business license.
② Take photos and upload certification photos (Photographic tool, ID card, dark pen and paper needed.)	② Provide the ID information of the legal representative
③ Provide payment information.	③ The legal representative take photos and upload certification photos (Photographic tool, ID card of the legal representative, dark pen and paper needed.)
	④ Provide payment information.

picture 3-11

The real-name verification for individual account is simpler and quite similar to the verification for company account. Therefore, the following part shows the details of real-name verification for company account.

First, input the company name, the unified social credit code or business license number and upload a clear business license color photo. Privately or individually-owned business cannot register for company account.

Second, input the legal representative name and ID number.

Third, prepare a photographic tool, ID card, dark-color pen, and a piece of paper for the verification of ID photo and finish this step within 15 minutes. The detailed

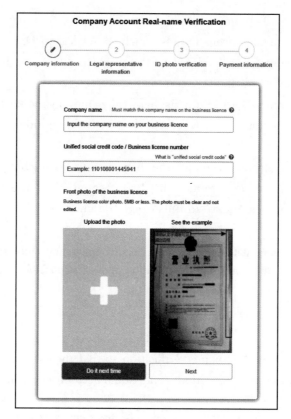

picture 3-12

picture 3-13

requirements for the ID photo are described in the following picture from Wish platform registration.

Then, upload the ID photo for verification. The detailed operation procedures to do this are provided in the following picture from Wish platform.

Finally, click 'next' to complete payment information. On Wish platform, detailed operation about how to add payment information is provided to ensure the user can

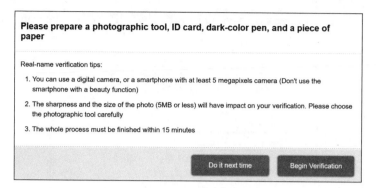

picture 3-14

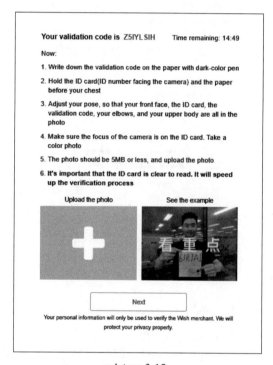

picture 3-15

receive money successfully from this platform after he/she begins business. This platform offers several payment service providers, like Payoneer and PayEco.

picture 3-16

If the user wants to receive payment through AllPay, he/she can choose AllPay from the pull-down menu like the following picture.

picture 3-17

After the payment information is confirmed, click 'Next' to submit the application. Then the user has completed all the registration processes and needs to wait for verification.

Questions

1. What will happen to the merchant's account if information provided for registration is not true or incorrect?
2. How many steps are involved in registering for a store on Wish platform? What are they?
3. What will be a secure and an insecure password like? Please write them down.
4. What factors should be considered in choosing a store name?
5. What should be provided for the real-name verification for company account?

Notes

API：Application Programming Interface，应用程序接口，是指一些预先定义的接口（如函数、HTTP 接口）或软件系统不同组成部分衔接的约定，用来提供应用程序与开发人员基于某软件或硬件得以访问的一组例程，而又无须访问源码或理解内部工作机制的细节；它也是一种中间件，用来为不同平台提供数据共享。

New Words and Terms

1. suspension	n. 暂缓；延期
2. freeze	v. 冻结
3. termination	n. 终止
4. entity	n. 实体
5. properly	adv. 正确地；恰当地
6. safeguard	v. 保护；保卫
7. penalty	n. 处罚；惩罚
8. token	n. 令牌；象征；标志
9. switch	v. 切换
10. digit	n. (0~9中的任何一个)数字
11. character	n. 字符
12. mark	n. 符号
13. infringe	v. 侵犯；触犯
14. certification	n. 证明；合格证
15. municipality	n. 直辖市
16. county	n. 县
17. photographic	adj. 照片的；摄影的
18. funds withholding	资金扣留
19. pull-down menu	下拉菜单
20. validation code	验证码
21. autonomous region	自治区
22. house number	门牌号
23. zip code	邮政编码
24. unified social credit code	统一社会信用代码
25. privately or individually-owned business	私营企业

Exercises

Task 3：Complete the following sentences with the words or phrases in the box.

suspension	termination	freeze	penalty	switch
infringe	properly	safeguard	photographic	certification

1. The court _____ their assets.

Unit 3 Opening a Cross-border E-commerce Store   53

2. Then he's not doing his job _____.

3. Both sides are now working towards a _____ of hostilities.

4. We successfully completed the _____ for open water diving.

5. You may face a reduction or _____ of benefits.

6. The industry has a duty to _____ consumers.

7. She worked as a librarian before _____ to journalism.

8. A backup copy of a computer program does not _____ copyright.

9. The software allows you to scan _____ images on your personal computer.

10. Withdrawing the money early will result in a 10% _____.

Task4: Register for a store on another Cross-border E-commerce platform and write down each step with pictures provided. Then compare the similarities and differences in registration between this platform and Wish platform.

Part C   Launching Products on a Cross-border E-commerce Platform

Different platforms have different rules, policies and procedures to launch products. However, there are some similar parts. This part will also take Wish platform as an example to show how to launch products on a Cross-border E-commerce platform.

1. Rules and policies for Launching Products

(1) Information provided during product upload must be accurate.

(2) Counterfeit products are strictly prohibited on Wish.

(3) Products and listings may not infringe on the intellectual property of others.

(4) Product listings may not refer customers off of Wish.

(5) Listing duplicate products is prohibited.

(6) Modifying a product listing from its original product to a new product is forbidden.

(7) Prohibited product listings will be penalized.

(8) A product listing may not include different products of high variance.

(9) Extreme price variance within one product listing is prohibited.

(10) Product listings that are detected to be misleading will be penalized.

(11) Extreme price increases within one product listing are prohibited.

For more and further information about product launching rules and policies, you can go to Policy Overview for merchants on Wish platform through this URL: https://merchant.wish.com/policy.

2. Procedures for Launching Products

As Wish platform merchants, they have three methods to launch products: add manually, add through a **CSV** product feed file, and add through an API. For new merchants on Wish platform, the first method is recommended to get them familiar with this platform and procedures. Therefore, the following content focuses on the detailed introduction of adding products manually.

First, log in to your merchant account at https://merchant.wish.com/login. From the top menu, click Products, Add New Products and then Manual. This will take you to https://merchant.wish.com/add-products.

picture 3-18

Second, enter the products' basic information including the product name, description, tags and unique product ID like the following picture. For the tags, you can add up to 10 tags for your product—the more tags, the easier it will be for users to find your product.

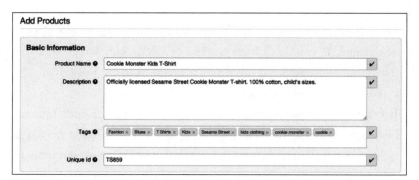

picture 3-19

Third, upload multiple high-quality images for each product which enables your potential customers to view your products as fully as possible and increases the exposure of these products.

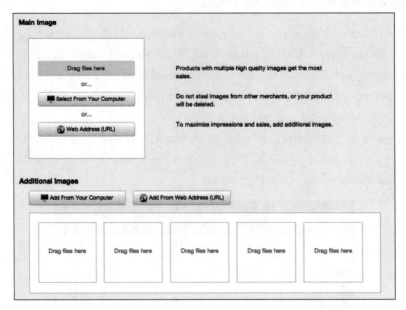

picture 3-20

There are three different methods to upload the images of products: Drag & drop, upload from computers and use image URL.

Drag & Drop: it is the simplest way to upload multiple images for your product. Click on the image you would like to add and drag it into the main image field. Meanwhile, you can continue to click the images you would like to add, and then drag them to additional image field.

Upload from computers: if you choose to add an image from your computer, first select 'Add From Your Computer' and then choose the images you would like to add for the product.

Use image URL: you can upload a product image via the web address by copying and pasting the image. If you don't have the image URL, you can go to a website where it's already listed and right-click on the product image to copy the URL.

Fourth, adding price and inventory.

You will enter the product's price, quantity, shipping costs and shipping time. You may also select a pre-set shipping time from the shown date ranges; or you may enter it manually if your shipping time is not listed. Fast and reliable shipping is crucial to customer satisfaction. The faster you fulfill and ship your orders, the more exposures your products will receive. Meanwhile, adding multiple high-quality images for your products is also one of the best ways to increase the product's exposure and push volume. The Local Currency is based on the Local Currency Code that can be found under Account → Settings → Currency Settings.

picture 3-21

Fifth, add country shipping. The country shipping of a product can be edited under the "Customize shipping price for chosen countries" section. Here you can set each country's shipping price and localized shipping price:

picture 3-22

Sixth, add colors and sizes. The best way to increase sales is to ensure your products have proper size and color information. Products that have correct sizing and color information sell more on the Wish platform. Customers trust products that have complete information about size and color options. They are much more likely to buy a product when they can select the size and color they prefer prior to the purchase. Luckily adding colors and sizes to your product is easy:

Simply check the box next to the color you would like to add. You may also add additional colors into the 'Other' field and it will appear in this section, for example,

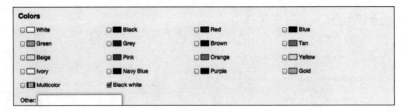

picture 3-23

Black & White. Adding sizes is just as easy:

picture 3-24

First select the type of product you are uploading. As you select the appropriate category, the size chart will adjust in order to show the appropriate sizing. Once you have selected the product category, click the boxes next to the sizes that you would like to list for this product.

Seventh, add product variations. It will auto generate product information you have entered:

Here, you can adjust the price and quantity of each variation. Let's say you do not have sizes for the multi-color. Simply adjust the quantity to 0.

Finally, add optional product attributes.

Add more information to your item, and expand the optional information section. Here, you can add the **MSRP**, brand name, landing page URL and **UPC**. Click on the corresponding field to add an attribute to your item. Now submit to upload your new product!

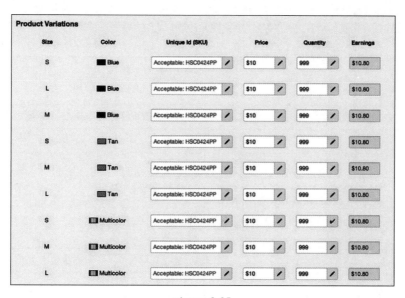

picture 3-25

picture 3-26

Questions

1. What are the rules of launching products on Wish platform?
2. What are the ways to upload the images of products?
3. What are the steps involved in launching products on Wish platform?
4. What are the ways to launch products on Wish platform?

Notes

1. CSV：Comma Separated Values，逗号分隔值，字符分隔值，其文件以纯文本的形式存储表格数据（数字和文本），是一种通用的、相对简单的文件格式，被广泛应用；其最普遍的应用是在程序之间转移表格数据。
2. MSRP：Manufacturer Suggested Retail Price，制造商建议的零售价，市场指导价，厂商建议的零售价。
3. UPC：Universal Production Code，通用产品编码，产品代码，条形码，是美国统一代码委员会制定的一种商品专用条码，并在 1949 年取得专利；是最早被大规模应用的条码，是一种长度固定、连续的条码，目前主要在美国和加拿大使用，后通行于国际贸易中。

New Words and Terms

1. counterfeit	adj. 假冒的；伪劣的
2. prohibit	v. 禁止
3. duplicate	adj./v. 复制的；复制
4. modify	v. 调整
5. penalize	v. 惩罚；处罚
6. variance	n. 变化幅度；差额
7. manually	adv. 手动地
8. tag	n. 标签
9. feed	n. 电子表格文件（包含产品信息等）
10. pre-set	adj. 预先设置的
11. corresponding	adj. 符合的；相应的；相关的
12. intellectual property	知识财产
13. drag & drop	拖曳
14. main image field	主图区域
15. additional image field	附图区域
16. copy and paste	复制和粘贴
17. push volume	推送量
18. prior to	先于；在…之前
19. landing page	（网站）登录页

Exercises

Task 5: Complete the following sentences with the words or phrases in the box.

| prohibit | counterfeit | duplicate | modify | manually |
| penalize | corresponding | variance | intellectual property | prior to |

1. Are you aware that these notes are _____.
2. A price _____ of 5％ is allowed.
3. For each rule that cannot be checked automatically, a drop-down list allows you to indicate that you checked it _____.
4. The war and the _____ fall in trade have had a devastating effect on the country.
5. New copies of the form can be _____ from a master copy.

6. Two students were _____ very differently for the same offence.
7. Smoking is strictly _____ inside the factory.
8. All the arrangements should be completed _____ to your departure.
9. The seats can be _____ to fit other types of vehicle.
10. A week earlier, it had been sued by Apple in a California federal court for violating a broad range of Apple's _____ rights.

Task 6: Get to know how to launch products on the platform you've registered in 3.3.1 Task 2, and compare and contrast the rules and steps for launching products between Wish and this platform.

Learning Aims Achievement and Test

Section	Opening a Cross-border E-commerce Store	Class hours		course credit	
Level	Medium	Capability	Be able to talk in English about the basic information covered in this unit concerning opening a Cross-border E-commerce store; Be able to register for a Cross-border E-commerce store; Be able to launch products on a Cross-border E-commerce platform	subtask	4
Number	Contents	Criteria			Score
1	basic concept	Be able to talk in English about the basic information covered in this unit concerning opening a Cross-border E-commerce store			
2	registration	Be able to register for a Cross-border E-commerce store			
3	Launching products	Be able to launch products on a Cross-border E-commerce platform			
4	differences and similarities in registration and launching products	Be able to understand the differences and similarities in registering and launching products on Cross-border E-commerce platforms			

Test and Comments	Score(1 point for each section)	
	Tutor Comments:	

Task Fulfillment Report

Title	
Class	Name	student ID

Task Fulfillment Report

1. Present your task and your plan for it.
2. Present the difficulties you came across on completing the task and your solutions.
3. Present what you have learnt through all this process.

Write a report with no less than 200 words.

Tutor comments:	Scoring Criteria(10-score range)	
	Attitude	
	Task Amount	
	Scoring Rules	

1. Timely finish all tasks.
2. Finish the tasks in reasonable way.
3. Reliable, coherent, logical and intelligible report.
4. Unfinished task will lead to 1 point deduction, and copy to 5 points deduction.

Keys

Text A

Task 1:

1. demanding 2. deposit 3. respective 4. verification
5. take...into consideration

Task 2:

1. 第三,商家需要比较不同的跨境电商平台,比如它们各自的特点、规则、优势和劣势,然后选择最适合的平台。

2. 由于疫情的影响,这些市场对于家用器具、娱乐产品和宠物用品的需求正在不断增加。

3. 第四,商家应该对于所选的跨境电商平台有一个系统的学习,尤其是关于注册、账户、商家服务条款、非法操作等,以此来节省时间和不必要的花销。

4. 对于亚马逊的注册来说,所需的材料包括企业营业执照,法人代表的身份证、邮箱、移动电话号码和VISA信用卡账户。

5. 你只需要将产品发送到特定国家的Shopee临时仓库,然后Shopee就会负责后续的配送工作,既省时又省力。

Text B

Task 3:

1. freezed 2. properly 3. suspension 4. certification 5. termination
6. safeguard 7. switching 8. infringe 9. photographic 10. penalty

Text C

Task 5:

1. counterfeit 2. variance 3. manually 4. corresponding 5. duplicated
6. penalized 7. prohibited 8. prior to 9. modified 10. intellectual property

Unit 4

Marketing on Cross-border E-commerce Platforms

Introduction

As that with traditional business, **the marketing mix** is very important for E-commerce. The 4P factors such as Product, Price, Place and Promotion are very for very important for online retailers and programs and activities such as **customer relation management** (CRM), and **brand awareness** promotion activities are also of great value to E-commerce sellers. However, without physical visiting to **brick-and-mortar stores**, E-commerce usually operates through the major E-commerce platforms and thus its marketing has its own emphases and rules.

Contents

Part A　Concepts Related to E-commerce
Part B　Store Profile and Product Listing Design
Part C　Promotion Activities
Supplementary Reading

Learning Aims

- Understand the features of marketing of E-commerce.
- Learn some basic tips for store description and product listing design.
- Learn some promotion activities for E-commerce.

Capability Aims

- Be able to design an online shop with the shop name, logo and main picture.
- Be able to upload a complete listing page with reasonable product description.
- Be able to use some promotion activities for online store.

Related Materials

Part A Concepts Related to E-commerce

Let us begin with the famous "**flywheel**" picture of Amazon and get down to some basic concepts for E-commerce, as picture 4-1 shows.

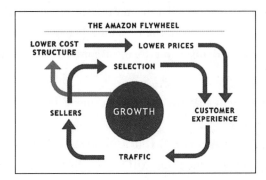

picture 4-1

Some basic concepts and ideas for E-commerce:

1. **Traffic**: Traffic means the number of visitors that a web page receives. For a website to be successful it needs traffic to be driven to it from various sources. This traffic, however, needs to come from people who will be interested in buying your product or service and in order for this to take place you need to target people within your niche.

2. **Exposure**: Exposure means presentation to view, especially in an open or public manner. In E-commerce, it also refers to the opportunity in which your products can be seen in the platform.

3. **Click**: Click tracking in E-commerce is essential due to its high importance in understanding how users interact with your content. Nevertheless, it is an indicator in analyzing your campaigns and it gives you a perspective on what visitors like, what makes them interact more and, finally, what drives up their actions to conversions.

4. **CTR (click-through-rate)**: CTR is a metric that measures the number of clicks a page receives divided by the total number of visitors browsing through that page.

5. **Conversion rate**: It means the percentage of user actions taken after total clicks on a display advertisement or other digital asset.

6. **Listing Page**: It is the product page for each of the items you sell on E-commerce platforms (especially Amazon). It is made up of the information you enter when you list your product including its title, images, description, and price.

7. **SEO** (search engine optimization): SEO is the process of making your online

store more visible in the search engine results pages (SERP). When people search for products that you sell, you want to rank as highly as possible so you get more traffic. You can get traffic from paid search, but SEO costs much less.

8. **P4P**: It is the term for "pay for performance" marketing on E-commerce products and sales. In AliExpress, it is called P4P or "外贸直通车" in Chinese.

9. **PPC** (pay per click): It is a form of online advertising where an advertiser will pay when a prospective customer clicks on an ad that is directed to the website of the advertiser. An example of a pay per click promotion platform is *Ad Words* from Google. Basically, it is paying for traffic rather than earning it organically through better search rankings for your site, or by doing some form of content marketing.

Questions

1. What is the most prominent feature of Cross-border E-commerce marketing compared to the traditional business?
2. Can you tell the relationship between traffic and conversion rate?
3. If you were going to sell products on AliExpress or Amazon, what would you do to increase the exposure of visibility of your products?

Notes

1. marketing mix:	营销组合(产品特征、价格、广告宣传方式以及营销地的组合，企业可调整这些项目以吸引消费者购买其产品)。
2. customer relation management (CRM):	客户关系管理，是指企业为提高核心竞争力，利用相应的信息技术以及互联网技术协调企业与顾客在销售、营销和服务上的交互，从而提升其管理方式，向客户提供创新式的、个性化的客户交互和服务的过程。
3. brand awareness:	品牌知名度，是指品牌为消费者所知晓的程度，也称品牌知晓度；品牌知名度反映的是品牌的影响范围或影响广度。
4. brick-and-mortar stores:	实体商店。
5. flywheel effect:	"飞轮效应"，大致描述了一家公司从好到卓越的转变过程；亚马逊公司提出其首要战略思路就是"飞轮战略"，即将其整个业务看作一个飞轮(飞轮非常重，不容易启动，但是一旦启动就会形成一股巨大的动能)，飞轮上的每一个要素协同发展，最终达成卓越的发展效果。
6. traffic:	网站流量，是指网站的访问量，用来描述访问一个网站的用户数量以及用户所浏览的网页数量等。
7. exposure:	曝光，该平台产品信息或公司信息在搜索结果列表或类目浏览列表等页面被买家看到的次数，有时也用 visibility 表示。

续表

8. CTR (click-through-rate)	点击率，点击率＝点击量/访问量，反映了该平台产品或公司在搜索结果页面是否足够吸引买家。
9. conversion rate：	转化率。
10. Listing page：	产品描述详情页面。
11. SEO (search engine optimization)：	搜索引擎优化。
12. P4P：	pay for performance，本意是绩效工资制，在跨境电子商务中指外贸直通车，是阿里巴巴会员企业通过自主设置多维度关键词，并对关键词进行出价竞争，从而获得免费展示产品信息的机会，以吸引买家点击产品信息，并且按照点击进行付费的全新网络推广方式。
13. PPC(pay per click)：	点击付费广告。

Part B Store Description and Product Listing Design

As is talked before, the aim of online store marketing is to increase the traffic and visibility, and thus, ultimately conversion rate and general turnover.

Let's begin with a picture (See picture 4-2). This is the homepage of AliExpress. AliExpress calls these flash banner pictures as display windows. The products in the display windows rank higher in search result. With the increased visibility, it has more chance to increase the traffic. AliExpress provides pay service to have the chance to get display windows for the eligible sellers, which they call as P4P (pay for performance). However, to be qualified for this program, the seller needs to achieve the required service rank, which means the seller has to maintain healthy performance target rates (i.e., order defect rate, late shipment rate, etc.) to prevent customers from having a poor customer experience.

Even though Amazon doesn't publicize its rules for search result page ranking, it is understandable to get the conclusion that sales volume and conversion rate should be two indicators of weight.

In this section, we will go down to two aspects to check the ways to increase the traffic and visibility. Namely, we are going to check: (1) some points to look out when laying out your visual store; (2) tips for designing the listing pages.

On finishing this part, you are expected to:
(1) complete your visual store profile with key elements.
(2) design a reasonable listing page for your favorite product.

1. Shop Profile

Your online store is your home base, where you showcase your brand, connect with

picture 4-2

your audience and ultimately sell your products. That is said, there are now many ways to reach and sell to existing and new audiences. However, it is very important to create an efficient shop profile.

The interfaces of the website and mobile terminals are different, but on your Shop Profile page, there are five key elements which will create a shop front that encourages shoppers to browse your shop.

(1) Shop logo.

Create a logo that represents what you sell.

For example, a shop that sells children's clothes can have a vibrant and playful logo. In contrast, a playful logo might not work for a shop that sells office wear.

(2) Shop name.

Choose a distinctive and memorable shop name that reflects your shop and products, while keeping with the platform's policy on shop naming.

(3) Cover photo.

When shoppers browse your shop, the cover photo is the first thing they see. Choose an image that captures the essence of your brand.

Avoid having text in your cover image. To get the best fit, use an image in 2∶1 aspect ratio.

(4) Images and videos.

Capture shoppers' attention with attractive images and videos showcasing your brand and products. Images and videos matter, as most of us respond to pictures and videos much more actively.

(5) Shop description.

Provide information about your shop, such as its history, type of products, shipping location, chat reply hours, and other unique qualities.

However, as many E-commerce platforms prescribe, you should not include personal information such as E-mail addresses or phone numbers to conduct transactions outside the platform.

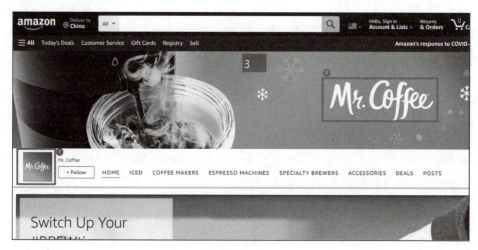

picture 4-3

2. Product Listing Design

2.1　What is the listing page?

An Amazon product listing is the product page for each of the items you sell on Amazon. It is made up of the information you enter when you list your product including its title, images, description, and price. Shoppers on Amazon use product listing pages to make a purchase, i.e., the Add to Cart button is on all product listing pages.

2.2　Basic Elements for a Listing Page

Here are two screenshots of an Amazon Listing Page. The basic elements include: (1)product title, (2)the main picture, (3)the fulfillment option (FBA or FBM), (4)the price, (5)the product description, detailed description, key words and the category that the product belongs to.

2.3　Tips for Listing Page Design

2.3.1　Product Images

The most prominent position of the listing page is held by the main photo, and thus it is extremely important for most ecommerce shoppers make a decision within just seconds on whether they want to further engage with a detail page or go back to search results.

Your main photo should clearly show what the product is before zooming in. It is better to produce a three-dimensional effect and thus helps people generate a rush to touch the product. It is worthwhile to mention here that Amazon <u>stipulates</u> that the background of the main photo should be pure white, and there is no such a rule for many domestic platforms and you'd better follow the prescription of the particular platform. For those platforms without such rules (Wish or AliExpress, for example), it is highly recommended to have your main photo reflecting the situation where the product can be applied.

Additional photos should provide additional angles of the product, or relevant lifestyle imagery. It is also probably worthwhile having one image of the 'back of the box' showing ingredients and instructions. Also, ensure the images are high-quality so the customer is able to <u>zoom in and out</u>.

In short, if it is <u>affordable</u>, you'd better have some professional photographers prepare for your photos.

2.3.2 Product Titles

For some cultural reasons, some Chinese E-commerce sellers are adapted for the Taobao way where they are apt to add some overlapped key words in the title to increase the visibility. However, it is not the case of English platforms, especially of Amazon.

Look at the best sellers in popular categories, and you will find that their titles usually consist of no more than 10-20 words. This is likely because customers have a hard time quickly scanning long titles, and they may even get annoyed with titles that are displayed this way (not to mention titles may get cut off while searching on mobile).

So, before posting your title, ask yourself the following questions.

- Does your title clearly describe to customers what the item is and if it is <u>compatible with</u> their needs?
- Does it mention the brand name?
- Does it clarify what the use case is or primary benefit?
- And most importantly, does it do all of this concisely so it isn't too long to skim?

For most titles, they can be put in this way: "the core key word ＋ brand name ＋ the secondary key word＋ modifier".

For example, a <u>succinct</u> yet complete title such as "Maximus Outdoor Indoor Hanging Pendant Lighting" probably works better than simply "Maximus Outdoor Light" or even than a 3-4-line long title that looks more like <u>spam</u> than a product title.

2.3.3 Product Descriptions

There are two most important parts of product descriptions. The first part is located on the right side of the main photo, usually with 5 points(Check it in picture 4-4). The second part is on the next page, usually called as detailed product description. The first tip about product descriptions is to make them concise and informative. Remember that customers are skimming, and so a 20-line long paragraph probably won't do the job. That means the seller should understand well the feature of his products and disadvantages of the competitive products.

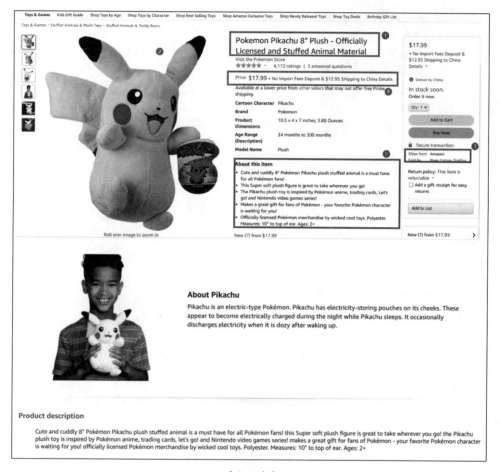

picture 4-4

Here are some contents you can put into the five points of product description:

a. The most prominent selling point A.
b. The most distinctive selling point B.
c. The size and quality of the materials.
d. When and how to apply the product.
e. Warranties.

One more piece of advice: Generalize these characters in a phrase and capitalize them at the beginning of each line. (Check the description in picture 4-5.)

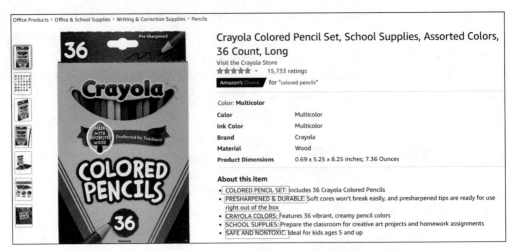

picture 4-5

For the detailed product description. Here is some advice.

Use your brand voice here and reiterate key selling points while mentioning any supporting facts that can help customers understand why they need to buy now. Here are the advised contents:

① Further after-sales guarantee.

② Detailed information about the product.

③ Supplementary feature without being mentioned before.

④ The free gifts and accessories.

In a word, strenuous work should be put to design listing pages, and you need continuously improve it with the change of key words rankings and holidays. Check that whether it is attractive enough to you. Only so can you attract the other potential buyers.

New Words and Terms

1. general turnover	总体营业额	
2. flash banner	活动广告条	
3. eligible	adj. 有资格的	
4. order defect rate	买家不良体验订单率	
5. late shipment rate	出货延迟率	
6. store/shop profile	店铺简介	
7. terminal	n. 终端	

续表

8. logo	n. （公司或组织的）标识，标志，徽标
9. vibrant	adj. 生气勃勃的；精力充沛的
10. essence	n. 实质；精髓
11. prescribe	v. 规定；命令
12. fulfillment options	订单履行（亚马逊上的商品常常有两种送货服务，一种是 FBA (fulfillment by Amazon)，即"亚马逊配送服务"；另一种是 FBM (fulfillment by merchants)，即"卖家自配送"）
13. stipulate	v. 规定；明确要求
14. zoom in and out	放大和缩小
15. affordable	adj. 付得起价格的
16. compatible (with)	adj. 可共用的；兼容的
17. succinct	adj. 简明的；言简意赅的
18. spam	n.（在网上）发（垃圾电子邮件）
19. capitalize	v. 用大写字母书写（或印刷）

Exercises

Task1：Choose a category and try to design a visual shop.

　　A：The category for your products：_____．

　　B：The Logo：

　　C. The shop name：_____

　　D. The shop description：_____

　　E. Try to describe the picture or the video that you are going to use for your shop frontpage.

（You can attach your picture in the blank and tell the reason why you choose it.）

_____

_____

Task2：Choose your favorite product and try to design a listing page for it. Write the five points description and the detailed description.

　　Description 1：

_____

_____

Unit 4　Marketing on Cross-border E-commerce Platforms　73

Description 2:

Part C Promotion Activities

Promotion is a great way to increase visibility and gain reviews. Here we are going to talk about some promotion activities, and you may find more when you actually run an E-commerce business. Lightning Deals, price discounts, best deals, coupons, buy-one-get-one offers, discount codes etc., are all great opportunities to offer and highlight a temporary discount to your product. This benefits you by not only allowing you to sell more units in a short amount of time, but also it temporarily lifts your baseline business.

1. Lightning Deals

Lightning Deals are flash sales that are featured on the Amazon Deal Page, one of the most frequently visited pages on Amazon. Not only do they help increase discoverability of your product, but they help you increase sales during the limited time sale and even after the deal is completed. This is because you often increase your rank and search relevancy due to the increased units sold during that flash sale, and this carries over for a period of time once the deal complete, sometimes for several weeks.

Lightning Deals for most sellers are invite-only in a sense since you can only run them when they show up on your "see all recommendations" section of the screen on Seller Central, and there is often a nominal cost associated with running this deal. For big events such as Prime Day and during the Holidays, Lightning Deals can be very successful in selling hundreds to sometimes thousands of units in a few-hour period, and also helping new customers discover your brand, even if they don't buy it immediately.

2. Drive External Traffic

Many brands forget about this part, or reserve all external channels to point to their online store. While there is of obvious value in directing traffic to your own site with ads, those same tactics will also work to promote your listings.

Strategically decide which channels make sense direct to the platform. For example, bloggers, vloggers, and other influencers often love directing traffic to Amazon because they can collect affiliate commission on any customers' purchases that come from their custom link. Video sharing social media, such as TikTok also work very well.

Amazon's new Influencer Program however has been developed specifically for social media influencers with large audiences. These programs can be highly beneficial to the long-term health of your business. Additionally, you can create discount codes to share externally such as on your social media channels to encourage customers to buy on Amazon, and hopefully leave reviews.

3. How SEO Works

Spend enough time searching for tips on how to optimize your E-commerce business and you are sure to come across dozens of SEO and keyword tools out there. Some of them promise hacks that are guaranteed to get you to a top ranking, and others say they 'trick' the search algorithm to feature your product first. While some of the tools come in handy in certain scenarios, what would be recommended is to approach SEO from the platform's viewpoint.

More than 80% of customers never scroll to page 2 of a search, so how can you ensure that customers are happy and continue to purchase? Only by providing relevant products that have a high possibility of converting into purchases.

A simpler interpretation: show customers products they want to buy. This factors in what keywords customers are searching for, conversion rates, related products, recent sales history, pricing, stock, and much more.

Thus, what keywords do you think customers are searching for when they are discovering your product? Have you included those terms in your keyword field when setting up your product (i.e. 'backend' keywords)? What products typically show up for your desired search terms, and how are they priced and how many reviews do they have relative to your product? How can you increase sales velocity in a short amount of time (i.e. promotion) so that you move up the rankings?

3.1 Write for Humans, Not Search Algorithms

Don't play the keyword stuffing game. Approach it from a customer's perspective on information they need to be convinced it's worth the purchase. Amazon has stated its mission is "to be Earth's most customer-centric company…" and that is a great way to approach incorporating keywords into your page contents rather than gaming the system with irrelevant keywords.

3.2 Enhanced Brand Content (EBC)

For sellers on Amazon, now available for brand registered sellers, EBC is a version of A+ content, which allows you more room on the page to add visuals and text to increase the customer engagement and tell a better product and a brand story. The potential benefits are increased conversion, lower return rates, and increased brand following. A+ content was originally only available to vendors but the recent roll-out to brand registered sellers is a huge opportunity for sellers to better showcase their products on Amazon.

New words and terms

1. Lightning Deal	闪购活动	
2. price discount	打折	
3. best deal	"聚划算"	
4. coupon	折扣券	
5. buy-one-get-one offer	"买一送一"活动	
6. discount code	折扣码	
7. affiliate commission	联盟佣金	
8. the search algorithm	搜索算法	
9. factor in	将……计入；把……考虑在内	
10. stuff	v. 填充；填塞	
11. EBC	enhanced brand content 是亚马逊提供给有品牌备案的卖家（brand registered sellers）的一种服务，可以在商品介绍部分看到更多的商品图片，商品更详细的功能的图片都可以放在这里，配合文字描述可以让商品页面更丰富，提升商品描述的视觉效果，好的图片能有效地帮助买家理解文字描述，让买家较快速地抓住商品重点，进而提高购买转化率	
12. A+ content	图文版商品详情页面，可以使用额外的图片和文本进一步完善商品描述部分；换句话说，如果你已经成功通过了亚马逊的品牌注册，那么从现在开始你就可以在商品描述页面添加图片和文字信息了	

Reading Comprehension

1. The following are benefits which promotions can provide EXCEPT _____.
   A. They help you sell more units in a short time
   B. They will increase your traffic in a short time
   C. They will surely bring about a higher conversion rate
   D. They usually are your rank and search relevancy

2. Which following platform EXCEPT _____ will help you to find a good influencer?
   A. Instagram   B. Amazon   C. TikTok   D. Quora

3. How do you make SOE work?
   A. You can optimize your key words with better understanding the need of your

potential customers
B. You can try to work with some online influencers to promotion your products
C. You can pay for some experts to hack the platform so that your products will rank high in the search page
D. You can improve the listing by understanding the search algorithm

4. What is indicated through launching of EBC program by Amazon?
A. Amazon will attach more value to the brand and intellectual property
B. Amazon will expand its distinctive service to more sellers
C. The tech will improve the buying experience
D. Visual function helps increase the conversion rate

Supplementary Reading

Buy Box on Amazon

If you have been selling on Amazon or have started researching becoming a seller, you have inevitably come across the term 'buy box'. The concept is simple, although the execution to manage it can be much more difficult.

Nearly every detail page has the option for other qualified sellers to also list their offer for that ASIN (Amazon's SKU identifier). So even if you are the manufacturer of a product, another seller could potentially undercut your price on the same item and be the default option on that detail page - or 'win the buy box'. The exception is for brands that have brand gating, which is extremely difficult to get approved.

picture 4-6

Thus, understanding the ins and outs of the Amazon **Buy Box** will always be a top priority for competitive third-party sellers, due to its high-impact on conversions. As there is no limit on the number of sellers or the amount of products that they can offer on Amazon's marketplace, the same product is often sold by many sellers, each competing for the maximum amount of sales.

The algorithm for who wins the buy box is proprietary, but the main components are price, prime eligibility, shipping cost, quantity, and the seller rating. As you can probably guess, price will have a major impact, but being Prime Eligible and having a high seller rating can sometimes be the difference between you winning or losing the buy box.

Aligning with Amazon's customer-obsessed mantra, the Amazon Buy Box was created in order to give the customer the best possible value for their money. It determines which product promises the best balance of high seller performance and low price.

Technically, each unique product should only have one ASIN (one UPC to one ASIN), but sometimes you will see several different listings for the same product, which is a confusing and frustrating experience for customers. Amazon continues to crack down on duplicate listings and gives brand registered sellers the ability to merge duplicate pages, so it's best to play by the rules and avoid looking for ways to create a separate page with less competition.

It is strongly commended that the sellers meet the below criteria:

1. Has an Amazon Professional Seller account.

2. Is "Buy Box-eligible," a status awarded to experienced sellers who have spent time selling on the Amazon platform and possess high levels of performance. This status was formally known as Featured Merchant and was visible to anyone. Any buyer or seller could see who was a Featured Merchant by looking at the Offer Listing Page for a particular product. Today, this information is only disclosed to the seller themselves in their Seller Central account.

3. Sell new items rather than second-hand. There is a separate Buy Box for used items.

4. Has available stock of the item competing for the Buy Box. Backordered items can now win the Buy Box, but the algorithm favors sellers that constantly have adequate inventory.

Notes

Buy Box:
亚马逊中的 Buy Box 是每一位商家都想要抢占的"黄金购物车",它位于单个商品页面的右上方,是买家购物时看到的最方便的购买位置;只要买家单击 Add to Cart 按钮,页面就会自动跳转到拥有这个 Buy Box 的卖家店铺。

Learning Aims Achievement and Test

Section	Marketing on Cross-border E-commerce		Class hours		course credit	
Level	Medium	Capability	Capability to launch reasonable online shop and products		subtask	4
Number	Contents	Criteria				Score
1	basic concept	Be able to tell the key elements of online marketing.				
2	shop profile	Be able to design an attractive online shop homepage.				
3	product listing	Be able to write a vivid product listing.				
4	promotion activities	Be able to tell the proper promotion activities for proper events.				
	Score (1 point for each section)					
Test and Comments	Tutor Comments:					

Task Fulfillment Report

Title	
Class	Name	student ID

Task Fulfillment Report

1. Present your task and your plan for it.
2. Present the difficulties you came across on completing the task and your solutions.
3. Present what you have learnt through all this process.

Write a report with no less than 200 words.

Scoring Criteria (10-score range)

Tutor comments:	Attitude	
	Task Amount	

Scoring Rules

1. Timely finish all tasks.
2. Finish the tasks in reasonable way.
3. Reliable, coherent, logical and intelligible report.
4. Unfinished task will lead to 1 point deduction, and copy to 5 points deduction.

Keys

Reading Comprehension: C, D, A, B

Unit 5
Market Research of Cross-border E-commerce

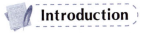 Introduction

According to Wikipedia, market research can be defined as "the process of gathering, analyzing and interpreting information about a market, about a product or service to be offered for sale in that market, and about the past, present and potential customers for the product or service; research into the characteristics, spending habits, location and needs of your business's target market, the industry as a whole, and the particular competitors you face."

Following this logic, E-commerce market research serves to inform retailers not only about their customers' needs and preferences but why consumers want to purchase certain products. By obtaining this kind of knowledge, merchants can effectively create the products, solutions and marketing campaigns that will increase their chances of online success.

In this unit, we are going to talk about some basic principles in selecting products and some rudiments of market research for E-commerce. Based on that, you should work out a proper way adapted to yourself.

Contents
    Part A   Basic Principle and Logic for Product Selection in Cross-border E-commerce
    Part B   Practical Methods of Market Research for Cross-border E-commerce
    Part C   Data Analysis for Cross-border E-commerce
    Supplementary Reading

 Learning Aims

- Tell the basic rules of product selection for Cross-border E-commerce.
- Understand some methods for market research of Cross-border E-commerce.
- Understand the indication of key factors in statistical analysis.

Capability Aims

- Be able to apply the basic rules to select products.
- Be able to present some products in view of one's own features.
- Be able to write a sales report with the help of the online tools of statistical analysis.

Related Materials

Part A Basic Principle and Logic for Product Selection in Cross-border E-commerce

Nowadays, when talking about Cross-border E-commerce, we usually refer to B2C business. It has been relatively easy to launch a virtual store and start a global business. However, there are many decisions to make and the first of all is to choose what to sell. It is said that selection far outweighs operation. If you choose the right product or <u>niche</u> and are well prepared before the coming trend, you may harvest a fat <u>profit margin</u>. While you try to follow some **trending products**, you may get a sound order number, but not so reasonable net earnings. If unfortunately, you choose inappropriate range of products, you may face <u>overstocked inventory</u> and a waste of money. There is no such thing as a normal routine when you do the selection. You should not depend on exclusively data analysis, but make the decision with <u>comprehensive</u> consideration based on a full understanding of your product and the target market.

Selling on E-commerce platforms and succeeding at this <u>venture</u> means targeting the best product categories and selling items that will empty out your inventory by speed. You have to carefully choose your products in order to make sales happen.

1. Basic Principle

The first and foremost rules for selecting products should always be these three: a) being lawful in both the country of registration and target market countries; b) <u>observing</u> the rules and regulations of the platform; c) being easy to pack and ship, especially for B2C stores. For Cross-border business, the shipment usually involves long time, and it is reasonable to choose products easy to store or carry, with long shelf time. However, apart from these, there are some other things to weigh. They are as follows.

1) It is better to choose products with simple operation. If you target the ordinary people, choose the product which is easy and simple to use. Otherwise, you risk all the troubles from after-sales service to refunding.

2) Fast-moving <u>consumer goods</u> should be a wise choice. A faster turnover will

bring about a higher profit and better fund utilization. If not, you should set higher profitability and choose products easy to promote by **word-of-mouth marketing**.

3) The supply-chain must be liable. Product sourcing is extremely important, if you are not a manufacturer. Many sellers chose **dropshipping** model in the early time, which now requires more techniques to deal with. It is highly commended to have solid cooperation with some factories.

4) There should be a potential market large enough. Even though there is usually fierce competition for such markets, the need of them is relatively huge so that there are reasonable profits for attendants.

5) There should be few dominant buyers. It is hard for the startups to enter the field if there exist several major buyers.

In short, you should keep close to your products and the market and react to changes immediately.

2. Self-Analysis

It is extremely important to know yourself before launching your categories. Think about these three aspects.

First, think about the supply source and ask whether you have any advantage geographically. For example, in China, there are industrial clusters with regional features, such as small consumer goods industry in Yiwu, wedding dress industry in Suzhou. These regional industrial clusters usually cover a huge range of products and offer competitive prices, with complete supply chains.

Second, think about the feature of your own team. Will you emphasize R&D or full range of products? Will you just focus a small group of products and target a niche market?

Third, evaluate your asset, especially cash. Allocate cash assets rationally. Unless you have a massive budget, you can't be the next **Best Buy** or Amazon. You have to niche down to run a profitable E-commerce store.

3. Positioning and Strategy

Based self-analysis, stores could decide their focus and the business strategy. As a seller, you have to think about your focus and the target market. It is especially important for the Cross-border E-commerce seller to know the target market, which influences the products a lot. For example, the most needed sizes of garments vary according different regions. Besides, you also need to decide the right E-commerce platform.

New Words and Terms

1.	rudiment	n. (某一领域)的基本原理/知识
2.	niche	n. 商机；市场定位
3.	profit margin	利润率
4.	overstock	v. 积压
5.	inventory	n. 库存
6.	comprehensive	adj. 全面的；详尽的
7.	venture	n. (有风险的)商业活动；投机活动
8.	observe	v. 遵守
9.	consumer goods	消费品
10.	utilization	n. 利用；使用
11.	niche down	细分；缩小
12.	garment	n. 服装

Notes

1. trending product：热销产品，电商有时喜欢称之为爆款。
2. word-of-mouth marketing：口碑营销，指企业努力使消费者通过其亲朋好友之间的交流将自己的产品信息、品牌传播开来。这种营销方式的特点是成功率高、可信度强。
3. dropshipping："代发货"，是外贸术语，是供应链管理中的一种方法。零售商不需要商品库存，而是把客户订单和装运细节发送给批发商，批发商将货物直接发送给最终客户，而零售商赚取批发和零售价格之间的差价。
4. Best Buy：百思买，是全球规模最大的家用电器和电子产品的零售、分销及服务集团。2011年2月，百思买宣布关闭在中国的全部9家门店，将在华业务交予五星电器打理。

Exercises

Task 1：Write a report to list the potential resources that can be leveraged, such as the nearby workshops, factories, agricultural products.

Task 2：Pick up among these resources the ones adapted to Cross-border E-commerce. (You can fulfill these tasks with the help of this table)

commodity	category	volume for each unit	easy to pack (or not)	shelf time
1.				
2.				
3.				
4.				

Part B Practical Methods of Market Research for Cross-border E-commerce

One feature of E-commerce market research is the application of big data. Sellers are able to take advantage of various tools provided by their platforms to track traffic and get access to different ratings. In this section we are going to talk about some practical ways to acquire valuable information.

1. Take Information from Buyer's Interface

1.1 Know about the Trending Products through Promoting Activities of the Platforms

Picture 5-1 is about the flash deals in AliExpress. The sellers attending such promotions need to meet some criteria. The products sold in Flash Deals usually are the trending products in their category. And you can use it for free.

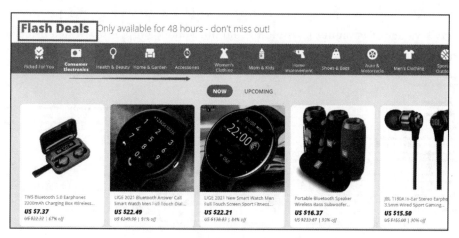

picture 5-1

1.2 Use the Related Key Words Offered by the Search Engine

When you put the key words in the search engine, it usually offers more specific **long-tail key words**, and these long-tail key words usually convey the real need of potential customers. Whenever a customer uses a highly specific search phrase, they tend to be looking for exactly what they are actually going to buy. In virtually every case, such very specific searches are far more likely to convert to sales than general generic searches that tend to be geared more towards the type of research that consumers typically do prior to making a buying decision.

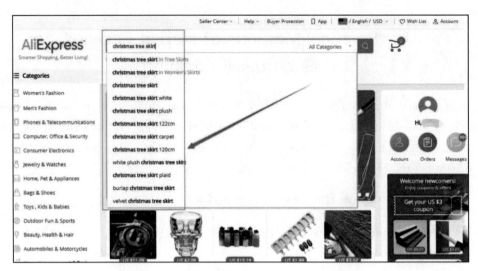

picture 5-2

1.3 Check Reviews and Find the Pain Points of Customers

The B2C platforms invite customers to write reviews about the product. Check these reviews and it is highly possible to find out some pain points, which offer you the opportunity to improve your products and develop your own registered brands.

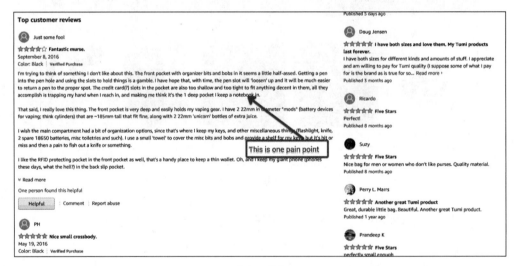

picture 5-3

1.4 Take Advantage of Tools Offered by Platforms

The platforms usually offer various tools for sellers to get hold of the information, for example, the best seller list. Read the best sold products and try to find some opportunities.

1.4.1 Research Amazon Best Sellers

The best-selling products in each category give you insights into what people are willing to buy.

From here, you can predict products that are likely to appeal to your target market for good conversion rates. Take a look and make a list of a few products that are exciting.

1.4.2 Amazon Most-Wished-for

One of the less known about E-commerce market research tools is Amazon's Most-Wished-for list. This website feature aggregates users' wish list data and shows interested parties precisely what people want the most, at a given time.

Through this tool, retailers can view the top 100 items in a plethora of categories, and then drill down even further by checking out the data compiled from subcategories.

picture 5-4

2. Uncover Trending Products through Social Media

Social media also provide valuable information. From Facebook to Instagram, YouTube to TikTok, you can drill on them and get a myriad of sales options.

Research Hashtags

If you have an interest in a particular industry, you can search for posts on it using hashtags.

Step 1: Use Hashtags for likes To Get Trending Hashtags

Hashtags-for-likes curates popular hashtags in different categories. While their specialty is **Instagram**, you can use the hashtags curated to search on other social media sites.

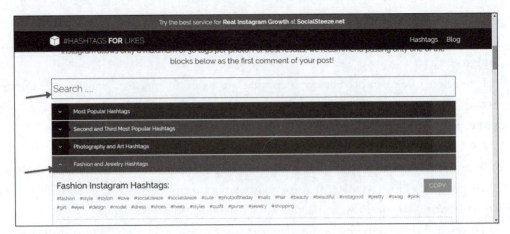

picture 5-5

picture 5-6

Step 2: Search for posts on Instagram Using Your Hashtags

Go on Instagram and search for posts with those hashtags. Using Instagram for product inspiration. Take note of interesting ideas and anything else that you like. Also, keep a list of those hashtags, they will be relevant for Instagram marketing later.

Step 3: Uncover Trending Posts on **Facebook** Using the Hashtags

Facebook has billions of active users. You'll get not just niche ideas here, but also insights into what your audience is willing to buy.

To start, type a keyword in the search area. You can use one of those hashtags you got in step one or an idea that you are considering.

You could filter the results. Ensure that you check out groups and Facebook pages for ideas into what people are interested in.

Bonus Tip-Posts with a lot of engagement - likes and comments - are signs that people are interested in that product. You can also check out those with fewer engagements for interesting ideas that you could modify later on.

3. With the Help of Third-party Tools.

There are a lot of third-party tools provided. You can use some for free but should pay for others. For example, you can use Google AdWords Keyword Tool to identify the keywords your audience is using to research products, services, solutions, and information related to this niche market. It is free and it offers lots of useful data related to these keywords, such as local and global search volume, level of competition, average **cost per click (CPC)** and more.

Another example is WatchCount. WatchCount shows the most popular eBay products. Using WatchCount is very easy. Your keyword could be your product idea.

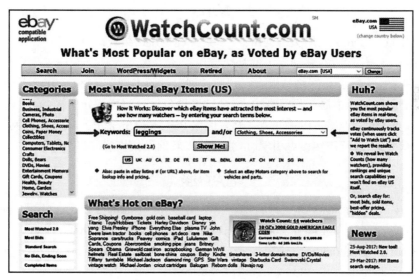

picture 5-7

You could also seek assistance from other tools such as Google Trends, Google Keyword Planner, etc. When you start doing such job, you may find that there are a lot of them.

New Words and Terms

1. criteria	criterion 的复数形式,(评判或做决定的)标准,准则
2. specific	adj. 明确的;具体的
3. generic	adj. 一般的;通用的
4. predict	v. 预言;预告;预报
5. aggregate	v. 合计为
6. plethora	a plethora of sth: 大量的某事物

续表

7. drill down	drill down/drill down on sth：向下钻取（指利用计算机获得更详细的资料）
8. myriad	n. 无数；大量
9. hashtag	（又写为 hash tag）社交媒体中使用的标签（关键词的一种），该标签无等级，又称"散列标签"
10. like	在网络媒体中，like/likes 表示"点赞"
11. curate	v. 管理；筛选；整理
12. filter	v. 过滤；筛选

Notes

1. Long tail keywords：长尾关键词由 3~4 个关键字短语组成。
2. Instagram：一款运行在移动端上的社交应用。
3. Facebook：一个社会化网络站点，译为"脸谱网"或"脸书网"，于 2004 年 2 月 4 日上线，总部位于美国加利福尼亚州门洛帕克，是世界排名领先的照片分享站点。
4. CPC：即点击付费（Cost Per Click，CPC，也称 Pay Per Click，PPC），是一种网络广告的收费计算形式，广泛用在搜寻引擎、广告网络以及网站或博客等平台。

Exercises

Task 3：Based on the tasks in Part A, try to select the products that could be popular or appropriate for Cross-border E-commerce. Write a report about that.

Task 4：Read the following product description and reviews, and write a report to improve the product or develop a new version.

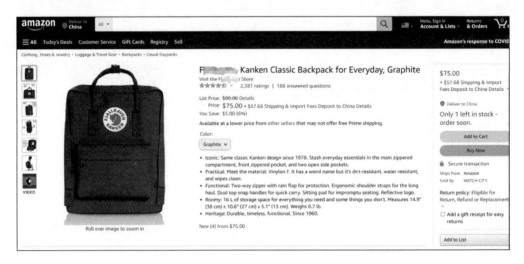

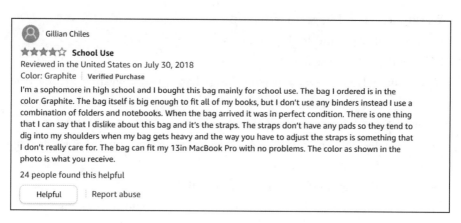

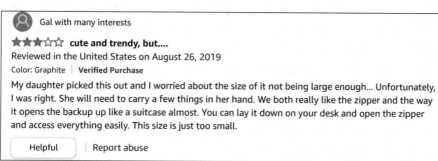

Part C Data Analysis for Cross-border E-commerce

One feature of E-commerce is that commercial websites install tracking tags on their pages to track events and observe customer behavior and these platforms provide sellers with various tools for data analysis.

Data analysis is not an exclusive method inaccessible to ordinary people. On the contrary, we use a lot of data analyses in everyday life. For example, we always compare our current weight with the past or with others'. So, it is easy to understand the use of data - we use data and data analyses to illustrate some facts and discover some truth.

1. Different Types of Data Analysis

Depending on the sophistication of your data analytics, you can conduct different kinds of analysis with your E-commerce data:

1) **Descriptive analysis** for revealing what's happen

This is the basic level of data analysis. It gives you an understanding of what happened in the past based on tracked events and additional data. Descriptive analysis can provide you with:

— A KPI (key performance indicator) dashboard.

— Weekly and monthly revenue reports.

— Overview of sales and lead generation.

2) **Diagnostic analysis** for understanding past events

This type of analysis shows you why things happen by revealing hidden trends and patterns in data and how they correlate with customer behavior. With diagnostic analysis, you can:

— Find out why you got a dip or peak in your revenue on the KPI dashboard by means of a data drilldown.

— Determine the most efficient marketing activity.

3) **Predictive and prescriptive analysis** for anticipating and forecasting

This is the professional league of data analysis. Predictive analysis helps you understand what's likely to happen if nothing changes. It shows you:

— How your sales will grow.

— Which leads are the most likely to convert.

— What risks you can decrease.

Meanwhile, prescriptive analysis based on sophisticated software and technologies helps you model the whole business in situations like a market change or turning off a whole promotion channel. In practice, you not only get to check any marketing hypothesis but also:

— Achieve top-level personalization.

— Improve the customer experience.

— Optimize product lines.

All of these levels of data analysis demand special tools. But even the most complicated E-commerce data analysis starts with the simplest tool for collecting and tracking data.

2. What You Have to Know to Get Started with E-commerce Data Analysis

First, let's take a helicopter view and look at the whole data analysis process. For various business, data analytics means creating sensible metrics that reflects the status of the business and getting insights on consumer behavior.

To make your data analysis meaningful, you need to:

(1) Make a table of contents.

(2) Understand what data sources and what kinds of data are available to you.

(3) Collect your data.

(4) Process your data.

(5) Clean your data.

(6) Data analysis... at last!.

2.1 Understand What Data Sources and What Kinds of Data Are Available to You

Get a whiteboard or open a new document and write down all your sources of customer behavior and advertising data: online chats, support forms, etc. Also, check out the formats this data comes in, paying attention to those services that don't have automated data export functions and don't have **APIs** (application programming interface) for integrating with your analytics tool. These services require more of your time and manual work, which isn't the best news.

At this stage, you have to define all the metrics that reflects the most essential business events and situations your business may find itself in as well as those metrics you want to measure in your analytics system.

2.2 Collect Your Data

This is the stage where a good technical setup will benefit your business. In fact, nowadays, you don't have to know things such as tracking tags, cookies, browsers, etc. A lot of data are available for sellers. You'll use all of it once you have enough experience.

picture 5-8

2.3 Process Your Data

Data processing means merging separate data streams into a single dataset and preparing this dataset for the next stage — data cleaning. During the data processing stage, the reliability of your data processing software means a lot.

2.4 Clean Your Data

Your data will be really "dirty" at the beginning — some data will get lost, some will be erased, some format conversions will go wrong, you'll learn to make backups, etc. You'll need to correct errors, delete duplicates, and heal your dataset to make it ready for data analysis.

If you skip this stage, all your previous and further work won't benefit your business. You'll just waste your time.

2.5 Data Analysis... at Last!

At this stage, all of your efforts will be repaid. But don't get us wrong: it's still a lot of work. You have to rely on your metrics system and see how it works with real revenue and cost data. This is the stage for reporting, visualization, shifting results, and finding insights.

Sometimes, analyzing E-commerce data makes your lives complicated. It's also true that the first fruit won't come fast. No matter how hard the way, you should tackle all the tracking, collecting, merging, cleaning, and reporting issues to become not only a successful E-commerce business but a data-driven one.

New Words and Terms

1. dashboard	n. (汽车上的)仪表板，一些数据可视化报告也使用这样的形式
2. anticipate	v. 预料；预期
3. hypothesis	n. 假说；假设
4. metric	n. 度量标准
5. dataset	n. 数据集
6. reliability	n. 可靠；可信赖
7. format conversion	格式转换
8. duplicate	n. 副本；完全一样的东西
9. visualization	n. 可视化

Notes

1. descriptive analysis：描述性分析，用于描述定量数据的整体情况，例如研究消费者对于某商品的购买意愿，可用描述性分析对样本的年龄、收入、消费水平等各指标进行初步分析，以了解和掌握消费者总体的特征情况。

2. diagnostic analysis：诊断性分析，描述性分析的下一步就是诊断性分析。通过评估描述性数据，诊断性分析工具能够让数据分析师深入分析数据，钻取到数据的核心。

3. predictive analysis：预测性分析，主要用于进行预测事件未来发生的可能性、一个可量化的值，或者是事件发生的时间点，这些都可以通过预测模型来完成。

4. prescriptive analysis：指令性分析，指令模型基于对"发生了什么""为什么会发生"和"可能发生什么"的分析帮助用户决定应该采取的措施。通常情况下，指令性分析不是单独使用的方法，而是在前面所有方法都完成之后，最后需要完成的分析方法。
5. API：即 Application Programming Interface，翻译为"应用程序编程接口"，是一些预先定义的函数，用来提供应用程序与开发人员基于某软件或硬件访问一组例程的能力，而又无须访问源码或理解内部工作机制的细节。

Reading Comprehension

1. When you need understand your performance and how your store goes, it is appropriate to make a _____ analysis.
   A. descriptive   B. diagnostic   C. predictive   D. prescriptive
2. Before make a marketing program, you'd better have a _____ analysis.
   A. descriptive   B. diagnostic   C. predictive   D. prescriptive
3. When you face a market change and try to optimize your product line, you need _____ analysis.
   A. predictive and prescriptive   B. descriptive
   C. diagnostic   D. all above
4. What should be done for cleaning data?
   A. setting sensible metrics
   B. building datasets with separate data stream
   C. deleting invalid data
   D. visualizing the trend with datasets

Supplementary Reading

Top Social Media Platforms

The number of social media websites seems to expand weekly. However, not all are retail <u>boon</u>. That said, the main ones that merchants can utilize to scale an E-commerce business are:

Facebook

For nearly every retailer, their audience is on Facebook. With the company housing 2.4 billion monthly active users, the odds that a brand's target audience is not present on the platform are almost nil.

Facebook gives retailers myriad of sales options to implement. With the ability to create a "Shop" tab on a business page, sellers can list a wealth of products, thereby allowing consumers to purchase merchandise directly from Facebook.

For retailers, this is a completely free feature that can generate tons of insights around clicks, views, purchases and more for each item.

This doesn't even mention the other Facebook E-commerce features to reach shoppers like granular targeting, tracking and advertising elements.

Instagram

Instagram (which is owned by Facebook) is another gargantuan sales opportunity for E-commerce businesses, touting over one billion users. Moreover, 59 percent of U.S. millennial use the platform.

Instagram's sales power is derived from its image-centric nature. With features like Shoppable Instagram posts, E-commerce retailers can tag the products shown in images. For instance, if a model is wearing a specific pair of sunglasses sold on the site, merchants can tag the item, highlighting its name, price and purchase link.

This is an essential feature for two reasons:

Before Shoppable posts, the only link brands could highlight were in their bio sections. Instagram data from Yotpo shows that 30 percent of users have purchased something they saw on the platform.

Features like Shoppable posts significantly streamline the purchase process for sellers on Instagram.

Check out this in-depth list of Instagram-specific marketing tools that you can utilize to boost your efforts.

Twitter

While the previously mentioned platforms dwarf Twitter, the company is still one of the biggest social sites online. Pew Research social media data shows that, in 2019, 22 percent of U.S. adult was on the platform, with 42 percent of them accessing the site daily.

While this may seem like a disadvantage, where Twitter shines for retailers is that they can generate clicks for literal pennies on the dollar. Since most E-commerce ads today are running through Google, Facebook and Amazon, there is less competition on Twitter, thereby making the ads less expensive to run.

While Twitter's audience may be smaller than other platforms, 22 percent of the nation's adult is nothing to scoff at when looking to generate traffic and sales.

LinkedIn

LinkedIn is essentially the professional version of Facebook. With over 575 million members, LinkedIn is the perfect platform for B2B organizations.

While users can run ads on LinkedIn, a more effective tactic for this platform is to drive E-commerce traffic by starting a group and providing relevant individuals with valuable information related to products or services.

Through this portal, sellers can dole out advice, promote webinars or similar events and potentially provide free samples or trials. That said, it is crucial to ensure that business owners only invite relevant individuals to a group and generate an apt name for the community that clearly communicates the topic at hand.

Additionally, if sellers are going to develop an active presence on this site, it is important to revamp the company's LinkedIn profile to help others learn about the brand and showcase the industry authority.

Pinterest

Pinterest is another image-based platform. With over 322 million monthly active users, Pinterest is a prime location for E-commerce retailers to marketing their goods.

This claim becomes quite apparent when examining Pinterest marketing statistics that show 40 percent of the platform's users earn an annual household income of ＄100,000. Moreover, those same statistics reveal that the average order value driven by Pinterest is ＄50, which is one of the highest for all social websites.

When speaking to promoted Pins, retailers tend to generate, as Pinterest reports, "＄2 in profit for every ＄1 the advertisers spent. When we looked at gross retail dollars instead of profit, that translated into a ＄4.3 return per dollar spent."

Additionally, Pinterest has made a conscious effort in recent years to become even more E-commerce friendly. The company's new "Complete the Look" feature is a "visual search tool that recommends relevant products in the home decor and fashion categories based on the context of scene. For example, if a user searches for a beach scene Pin, the platform will recommend products found in similar images such as hats, sandals and sunglasses. As a result, brands will potentially gain more exposures on Pinterest as more of their Pins are surfaced via visual search."

Pinterest is a fantastic platform to grow a brand through social commerce.

Snapchat

Once the underdog of social media websites, Snapchat has earned its place among the most prominent online destinations in the world.

For brands that target a younger audience, Snapchat is a premier location with the service touting 16.4 million users between 12 and 17-years old.

In terms of its E-commerce capabilities, the company launched a variety of ad options in late 2018, enabling retailers to highlight collections and product catalogs, utilize pixel targeting and take advantage of other significant E-commerce-focused elements.

New Words and Notes

1. boon	n. 非常有用的东西；益处	
2. gargantuan	adj. 巨大的；庞大的	
3. tout	v. 兜售；招徕	
4. millennials	本来指"千禧世代"，也称"Y 世代"，这个名词被公认为在 20 世纪的最后一个世代诞生成长的人，进入青年期后，2000 年就过去了	
5. bio section	Instagram 上的个人标签页面	

续表

6. Yotpo	一家来自以色列的创业公司,主要以 B2B 的形式,通过对 UGC 评论内容的抓取,再通过多渠道的传播帮助企业进行营销,其主要客户以美国为主,遍及欧洲和以色列
7. dole out	分发;发放
8. webinar	网上研讨会;在线会议
9. revamp	v. 翻新

Learning Aims Achievement and Test

Section			Class hours		course credit	
Level	Medium	Capability			subtask	5
Number	Contents	Criteria				Score
1	rudiments	Be able to tell basic logic for product selection				
2	market research	Be able to get inspiration from reading reviews				
3	market research	Be able to get ideas through tools provided by platforms				
4	data analysis	Be able to understand functions of different data analysis				
5	data analysis	Understand the general steps of data analysis				
Test and Comments	Score (1 point for each section)					
	Tutor Comments:					

Task Fulfillment Report

Title				
Class		Name		student ID
Task Fulfillment Report					

1. Present your tasks and your plan for it.
2. Present the difficulties you came across on completing the task and your solutions.
3. Present what you have learnt through all this process.

Write a report with no less than 300 words.

Keys

Reading Comprehension: A,B,D,C

Unit 6

Cross-border E-commerce Customer Service(Ⅰ)

It is acknowledged that customer services do exist during the process of purchasing and it always plays a significant role in the period of pre-sales service, in-sales service and after-sales service. For E-commerce, custom service in this field does have its distinctive features and usually covered with a color of high-tech. For customer service representatives in charge of E-commerce platforms, there are no facial expressions and obvious gestures to read. They only have their knowledge, skills, expertise, and some data to rely on when approaching a customer and estimating their needs and the outcome. In this unit, we will talk about general types of customer services including the factors affecting customer experience and search for communication skills to keep your customers satisfied.

Contents:

Part A An Introduction to Customer Services and Factors Affecting Customer Experience

Part B Rules and Features of Cross-border E-commerce Customer Service

Supplementary Reading

 Learning Aims

- Learn about the types of customer services and the factors affecting customer experience.
- Understand the features of customer service in E-commerce.
- Learn about the problems customers usually complained and the solution to keep customers satisfied.

- Be able to identify types of customer services and understand the factors affecting

customer experience.
- Be able to design the customer service procedure for E-commerce.
- Be able to detect the real problems of customer complaints.

Part A An Introduction to Customer Services and Factors Affecting Customer Experience

In order to gain a satisfied business reputation, customer services are as important as sales, although it does not produce any revenue for the company. And it certainly increases sound reputation of the organization in the markets and among the customers. In this article, we firstly talk about types of customer sales services.

Normal work of customer services seems easy but not simple. It is about communicating with customers online at working time in order to deal with all the problems to keep customers satisfied. For example, on Amazon, online communication between sellers and buyers often goes through messages in E-mail.

1. The Major Type of Customer Service

First of all, what are the major types of customer services? Generally speaking, it contains three types which are pre-sales service, in-sales service and after-sales service. In each type, the customer service's duty and responsibility are different.

(1) To deal with the problems and improve the sales in **pre-sales service**.

We have explanations for the first purpose. Staff members who work for this service need to have related professional business knowledge, know the features of each product and get familiar with the process of when and why customers need to buy this product. In some time, they even must have some necessary sales negotiation skills when customers want a bargain. Anyway, pre-sales customer service needs to provide customers with product information from a professional perspective and recommend customers a best item fit with their needs and push customers to make orders and payment in right time. So, the sales will be up finally.

(2) To improve customer experience in in-sales service.

The purpose of **in-sales service** is to provide the buyers with logistics information and communicate with buyers instantly before the goods start to deliver. If anything goes wrong to lead to the delay of delivery, customers will be informed as soon as possible through in-sales services.

(3) To deal with problems and avoid goods return in after-sales service.

Most of us think that **after-sales service** is more important than the previous two ones. To some extent, it is reasonable because customers comment to purchased products and logistics would affect the reputation of one online-business. Sometimes if the goods have quality problems or the buyers want a return and refund, the service provider must have the ability to deal with these problems. There are some satisfying solutions such as gifting the customers coupons or discounts to keep a good reputation for the business trade. In a word, to deal with public relations crisis and to reduce the loss is the ability to run after-sales services.

After learning about the types of customer services, the significance of pushing all three sales services' abilities is to improve the customer's experience. Therefore, what are the reasons and **factors to affect customer experience**? Usually there are two layers to be separated. One is about the reasons to push customers to make orders and the other is about the reasons to hinder customers to make orders.

2. The Factors Pushing Customers to Buy

2.1 The Image Quality

When shopping online, beautiful and clear pictures are the main factors to push buyers to make an order, and the beauty of the pictures and the details of the goods are also what buyers pay attention to. Overseas buyers particularly prefer to see real pictures because these real pictures stimulate buyers' true feelings in purchasing.

2.2 The Buyers Comments

Research shows that more than half of buyers check the buyer reviews before making an order. In after-sale work, guiding buyers to leave positive reviews that can effectively improve the **conversion rate of goods**.

2.3 The Buyers Show

Positive buyer shows can directly influence buyer decisions, which is similar to the effect of buyer reviews mentioned earlier. Sometimes in order to collect more excellent photos of buyers, merchants will launch some activities in the form of giving gifts to attract more buyers to provide photos show.

2.4 Comparative Price of Similar Products

The online display makes the price comparison easier. For sellers, if your product is also sold by other sellers on the same platform, the seller is advised to do a good job of differentiation. Even if it is just a visual difference, you'll get a higher conversion rate for the product you're selling.

2.5 Instant and Effect Communication

Addressing customer questions instantly can promote customers to order as soon as possible. A delayed response may solve the problem, but while the customer is waiting, he or she may find a new seller. If you cannot reply to the message in the first time due to the time difference, you can explain to the customer.

3. The Factors Hindering Customers to Buy

3.1 Shipping Not Free

At some time, although free shipping is included in the total price, there is a big difference between the experience of free shipping and not free shipping for buyers. Sellers are generally advised including shipping costs in their pricing.

3.2 Too Slow in Logistics

Although the problem of slow Cross-border logistics speed can be solved by overseas warehouse delivery, sometimes in the absence of overseas warehouse, it is necessary to select a reasonable logistics company to improve the speed of logistics, especially during the time of big promotion activities, when logistics is easy to burst in warehouses. At this time if you choose to deliver the goods at a certain probability it will be delayed.

3.3 Troubles in Payment

There are possibilities to cause troubles in payment. Some overseas buyers are not good at using the Internet. Internet speeds are slow in some areas. Banking payment systems in some countries are not easy to use. There are many reasons why a buyer cannot make a successful payment. So, ask the buyer if he or she is having trouble paying and trying your best to give assistance is always better.

3.4 Complex of Return and Refund

The picture of the goods is too different from the real ones, the quality of the goods or the buyer's requirements are not met, and all these situations will lead to the return of goods. But Cross-border E-commerce is expensive to return goods. Buyers could pay several times more to return goods to the seller than the price of goods. These issues make the return process complicated. It is suggested that competent sellers consider overseas warehouse delivery to reduce the cost of returning goods and reduce the buyer's concerns.

In summary, we learn all the factors to affect customer shopping experience and please remember that it is important to improve customers' satisfaction through taking measures.

Questions

1. What are major types of customer sales services?
2. In your words, can you summarize the factors improving customer shopping experience?
3. In your words, can you summarize the factors hindering customer shopping

experience?

New Words and Terms

1.	gain	v. 获取，争取
2.	reputation	n. 名声，声望
3.	revenue	n. 收入
4.	perspective	n. 角度，视角
5.	gift	v. 赠予
6.	layer	n. 层面，层次
7.	push	v. 推动，促使
8.	hinder	v. 阻碍
9.	stimulate	v. 刺激，促使
10.	display	n. 陈列，展示
11.	platform	n.（购物）平台
12.	differentiation	n. 差异化
13.	promote	v. 提升
14.	competent	adj. 有能力的
15.	concern	n. 担忧，顾虑
16.	working time	工作时间
17.	sales negotiation skills	销售谈判技巧
18.	delay of delivery	物流延迟
19.	customers comment	客户评论
20.	public relations crisis	公关危机
21.	reduce the loss	降低损失
22.	positive reviews	有效评价
23.	in the form of	以……形式
24.	visual difference	视觉差异
25.	time difference	时差
26.	free shipping	免运费
27.	total price	总价
28.	shipping costs	运费
29.	logistics speed	物流运输速度
30.	promotion activities	促销活动
31.	banking payment systems	银行支付系统

Notes

1. prep-sales service：售前客服，需要具备专业的商业知识，了解每件商品的特点，并且熟悉买家下单的操作流程，以及具备一些必要的销售谈判技巧；售前客服通常需要解答客户对商品、服务和物流的咨询。
2. in-sales service：售中客服，主要任务是为买家提供物流信息，在发货后的第一时间和买家进行即时沟通，告知买家物流服务跟踪单号，以及预计可以送达的时间；如果遇到特殊情况导致物流延迟，客服应及时、主动联系买家说明情况，促使销售流程正常进行。
3. after-sales service：售后客服，通常负责处理买家收到货以后的事宜，引导买家给商品留下好评，并对店铺和物流服务进行有效的评分；这些措施都对一家网店的销量和名誉有好处；如果卖出的商品出现质量问题，或者买家对商品不满意想要退货退款，那么客服需要有一定的应变能力；在这种情况下，客服可以适当给予优惠或部分退款等措施，既让买家满意，又要权衡利弊，尽量减少损失；总之，售后客服需要经常面对买家情绪不好的情况，这就要求客服具备处理危机的能力，擅于安抚买家情绪，能积极解决纠纷。
4. factors affecting customer experience：影响客户体验的因素，这里主要从正反两方面来说明；第一类是促使客户满意的因素，第二类是阻碍客户满意的因素。
5. conversion rate of goods：商品转化率，这里指提高商品销量。

Part B Rules and Features of Cross-border E-commerce Customer Service

1. Rules of Customer Service in E-commerce

There are "4P"s to achieve a good customer service in E-commerce.

1) Promptness：Timely attention to issues raised by customers is critical. Requiring a customer to wait in line or sit on hold sours an interaction before it begins.

2) Politeness：Saying "hello" "good afternoon" "sir/madam" and "thank you very much" are a part of good customer service. For any business, using good manners is appropriate whether the customer makes a purchase or not. Some platforms provide standard greeting models such as Alibaba Group and JD.com.

3) Professionalism：All customers should be treated professionally, which means the use of competence or skill expected of the professional. Professionalism shows the customer they're care for.

4) Personalization：Using the customer's name is very effective in producing loyalty. Customers like the idea that whom they do business with knows them on a personal level.

2. Distinctive Features of Customer Service in E-commerce

While the aim and basic rules of customer service for E-commerce are the same as those of traditional business, the ways to reach the goal are somewhat different. A very prominent feature of customer service is the application of technology. We can look into it beginning with customer relationship management.

2.1 Customer Relationship Management

According to Investopedia, customer relationship management (CRM) refers to the principles, practices, and guidelines that an organization follows when interacting with its customers. From the organization's point of view, this entire relationship <u>encompasses</u> direct interactions with customers, such as sales and service-related processes, forecasting, and the analysis of customer trends and behaviors.

CRM is often used to refer to technology companies and systems that help manage external interactions with customers. Major areas of growth in CRM technology include software, cloud computing, and artificial intelligence.

Elements of CRM range from a company's website and emails to mass mailings and telephone calls. Social media is another way companies adapt to trends that benefit their bottom line. The entire point of CRM is to build positive experiences with customers to keep them coming back so that a company can create a growing base of returning customers.

Special CRM software <u>aggregates</u> customer information in one place to give businesses easy access to data, such as contact data, purchase history and any previous contact with customer service representatives. This data helps employees interact with clients, <u>anticipate</u> customer needs, recognize customer updates and track performance goals when it comes to sales. However, for successful CRM, companies must learn to <u>discern</u> useful information and <u>superfluous</u> data and must <u>weed out</u> any <u>duplicate</u> and incomplete records that may give employees inaccurate information about customers. Moreover, industry analysts are increasingly discussing the impact that artificial intelligence applications may have on CRM.

In short, as a very important part of CRM, customer service should be probed in this larger background.

2.2 An Omnichannel Strategy

Besides the widespread application of technology by E-commerce platforms and sellers, the customers are more adapted to new approaches in the information age. Nowadays, customers make their purchasing decision through multiple channels such as websites, social media, email, phone, etc. It's reasonable for E-commerce sellers to build an <u>omnichannel</u> strategy to identify the pain points of the customers and understand the potential customers better.

It is understandable that CRM systems start by collecting a customer's website, email, telephone, and social media data — and more — across multiple sources and channels. It may also automatically pull in other information, such as recent news about the company's activity, and it can store personal details, such as a client's personal preferences on communications. For sales, your CS agents can work faster and smarter with a clear view of their pipeline and <u>accomplish</u> more accurate forecasting.

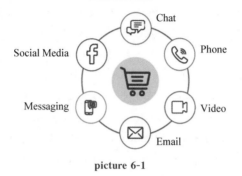

picture 6-1

2.3 Various Useful Tools in Information Age

2.3.1 A Shared Inbox

It is highly advisable for online sellers to set up **"a shared inbox"** that could integrate the E-commerce platform. That shared inbox would enable the whole team to keep up with customer requests and stay organized.

2.3.2 A Knowledge Base

To set up a knowledge base that enables potential customers help themselves. Try to deal with this point culturally. In China, shoppers are accustomed to contact sellers directly. The same happens in East Asia. However, in North America, there are more online shoppers who want to help themselves than you expected. Picture 6-2 shows the number of people in North America who want to solve the problem before contacting customer service. It is sound to always keep the FAQ(Frequently Asked Questions) reserve well prepared.

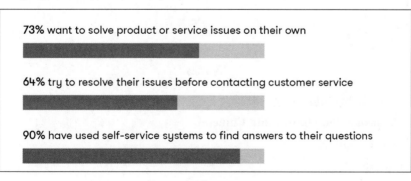

picture 6-2

Data from 80 Customer Service Statistics: 8 Lessons to Fuel Growth in 2019 and Beyond

2.3.3 Personal Touchpoints and Customer Support Channels

<u>Automation</u> is trending in E-commerce world. Some say AI (artificial intelligence) could work very well for customer service such as automatic reply. However, it is very important not to lose the personal touch in the process.

E-commerce businesses can offer support to their customers through a call center, live chat, and other channels. However, for many small online sellers, live chat and email are much more reasonable and reliable tools.

The real-time support channel such as live chat can significantly reduce the cart abandonment and increase sales when used well. However, some platforms just forbid direct communication between sellers and shoppers. For example, Amazon just <u>prohibits</u> direct contact between them and only the E-mails within the platform are permitted. Wish, the largest mobile E-commerce platform in North America has the same rule, too.

In short, there are various tools provided to improve your customer service level. Take advantage of all assistance well and properly and they could be very helpful.

New Words and Terms

1. encompass		v. 包含,涉及
2. aggregate		v. 汇集,聚集
3. anticipate		v. 预计,预料
4. discern		v. 识别,察觉
5. superfluous		adj. 多余的,过剩的
6. weed out		剔除,淘汰
7. duplicate		n. 复制品,副本
8. omnichannel		adj. 全渠道的,多渠道的
9. accomplish		v. 完成
10. automation		n. 自动化
11. prohibit		v. 禁止

Notes

a shared inbox:这里指共享的电子邮件收件箱。

Exercise 1. Translate the phrases into Chinese

1. competitive advantage: _____

2. conversion rate: _____

3. brand awareness: _____

4. cloud computing: _____
5. artificial intelligence: _____
6. returning customer: _____
7. live chat: _____
8. cart abandonment: _____

Task 1: Think about the possible situations that may involve customer service and support for an online store, and try to write them down.

Exercises 2. Please use the words and expressions in the box to complete the sentences below about general descriptions of customer sales services.

involves	anticipated	moderate
gratitude	take the initiative to	put yourself in their shoes

1. Cross-border E-commence customer service staff need to show _____ to customers at all times.
2. Business people believe that if they _____ get more new skills, there will be a better job available to them.
3. The only capital investments plan _____ new office space and the equipment needed for that space.
4. Customers would really appreciate it if you could _____ to tell them how to deal with this return dispute.
5. The transaction value of China's Cross-border E-commence is _____ to reach 20.3 trillion yuan in 2021.

Exercises 3. Please fill in the blank with the correct form of the given word.

1. Negative reviews include those complaining that the actual products do not match the photos or the delivery is _____. (delay)
2. E-commerce is all about _____. (reputable)
3. Respond to the comments politely and show your _____ (appreciate) for positive reviews.
4. More positive reviews can neglect impacts and leave new buyers with a better _____. (impress)
5. A damaged online reputation can undermine your other efforts in _____ (promote) and marketing.

Exercises 4. Please learn the following words in the box and choose the most appropriate one to fill in each blank.

handle	unable	request	unsatisfactory
agreement	include	recommend	supplier

How to reply to a refund request? While most issues can be handled successfully through a basic open dialogue between the supplier and the buyer, sometimes certain situations must be turned into more formal _____. We advise that the _____ and the buyer to do their best to discuss issues with each other and come to communication during the Open Dispute process. If the supplier and the buyer cannot reach an _____ during the 15-day Open Dispute time period, the buyer may pursue the complaint. By filling a claim, the buyer states he or she is _____ to reach a reasonable agreement with the supplier, and is requesting the platform to step in to _____ the matter. Reasons to pursue the complaint may be different. They can _____ the supplier not responding to the buyer's requests or refusing to partially refund the buyer for an order sent back in an _____ condition.

Supplementary Reading

How to Handle Some Real Difficult Scenarios in E-commerce Customer Service

When you are in customer service and support, you may be caught in some very hard scenarios. Here are some tips for you to cope with these difficulties.

1. The Customer Wants You to Bend the Rules

Most requests from customers are reasonable, and every effort should be made to make them happy.

Bob Farrell describes this as "giving them the pickle," a phrase which refers to a letter he received from an unhappy customer who wasn't able to get an extra pickle for his hamburger. Fulfilling a small request can often leave a positive impact on a customer, which is why it's almost always worth it to just "give them the pickle."

But what about requests that you truly cannot say yes to?

I can give you a very candid story of when this really mattered to me: I was checking in to a hotel with a few of my friends, one of whom had a severe allergy to cats. I vividly remember watching a couple plead with the front desk employee to let their cats stay (the policy was "No Pets").

If the front desk employee had given in to their request, he would have (unknowingly) made our group upset, trading one potentially unhappy customer for an even bigger problem.

I remember being impressed with how he handled the situation, and I'll paraphrase his response below:

"As much as I like fulfilling our customers' requests, I'm afraid that the 'No Pets' policy we have in place is too important because it impacts the safety and comfort of other customers. Can I perhaps call around for locations where your cat might be able to stay?"

It was a stellar response to a pretty wacky request; after all, pet owners should know to check a hotel's pet policy before booking a room.

Remember that a customer's perception of your service quality is greatly affected by how attentive, thoughtful, and sincere you are. In an awkward scenario where you simply have to refuse a request, showcasing your empathy and willingness to find an alternative is one of the best ways to lessen the sting of saying no.

2. The Customer Is Extremely Angry

Support champions are often required to act as lightning rods, to take the brunt of an emotional, angry customer despite the fact that it is not their fault.

Sometimes, this anger from customers is unjustified; other times, they have a cause for their actions. Either way, it's often quite hard to win back an extremely angry customer.

However, the smart folks at Telephone Doctor have a great system called "ASAP" for dealing with the most difficult of customers:

Apologize sincerely: "I'm sorry" is a mandatory response in these situations, even if it isn't your fault. Consider your "I'm truly sorry about that" as a personal apology to the customer that the experience wasn't up to their expectations — not that you are to blame.

Sympathize: Many times, angry customers are just as interested (if not more interested) in hearing that someone empathizes with their situation over getting the actual problem fixed. Even if you cannot understand why a customer is so angry, you can imagine how you'd like to be treated if you happened to be that upset. Even small phrases like "I understand how upsetting that must have been" can have an impact on getting the customer to realize that you're on their team in this pursuit to make things right.

Accept responsibility: As the ambassador of your company, you accept responsibility for the customer's unhappiness. Again, this doesn't make you at fault — and it doesn't give the customer leeway to demand whatever they want — but it does give them someone to talk to instead of being angry at a faceless company.

Prepare to help: With angry customers, the actual "fix" tends to take up a small portion of the entire support process. Placing a replacement order likely takes you very little time, but that fix doesn't address the underlying problem of the customer's frustration and unhappiness. These emotional fixes are often the most important element: refunding someone may take you 15 seconds, but did you make sure enough time was spent trying to help them calm down and leave happy?

It's hard to come up with a perfect solution for a customer in this state, and know that even if you handle things perfectly, some people simply cannot be appeased. But don't let that stop you from making your best effort.

3. The Customer Is Abusive

An abusive customer and an angry customer are not the same thing. An abusive customer is someone who has clearly crossed the line and is mistreating you.

Shut it down, no exceptions. But don't lose your cool; you must notify leadership so they can commit to a swift, immediate action. <u>Loop someone</u> else <u>in</u> — a support lead or other team leadership. Do not handle this situation yourself.

The leader should cancel the account and tell the customer not to contact you or anyone else on your team again:

> This is John Smith, CEO.
>
> I'm stepping in to let you know I've followed this conversation since the beginning. Given how it's played out, it's best that we part ways. The members of my team deserve to be treated with respect, and I haven't seen that in this exchange.
>
> I've canceled your account and refunded you for the rest of the month. You will not be able to reactivate the account.
>
> John

Nobody enjoys these situations. They're a mess. But the chances of not running into something similar over years or decades of experiences are slim, so be prepared.

New Words and Terms

1. stellar	adj. (informal) excellent 优秀的；精彩的	
2. wacky	adj. 古怪的，荒诞的	
3. showcase	v. 充分展示	
4. empathy	n. 同感，共鸣	
5. alternative	n. 可供替代的选项	
6. lighting rod	又称 lightning conductor, 避雷针	
7. brunt	n. 冲击力	
8. mandatory	adj. 强制的；法定的	
9. leeway	n. 自由活动的余地	
10. loop sb in	v. 把……拖进……圈子	

Think: How to refuse some unreasonable requests from some customers.

Learning Aims Achievement and Test

Section	Cross-border E-commerce Customer Service (I)	Class Hours		Course Credit	
Level	Medium	Capability	Be able to understand the importance and rules of Cross-border E-commerce through English Reading	Subtask	3
Number	Contents	Criteria			Score
1	Identification and understanding	Identify and understand types of customer services and factors to affect customer shopping experience			
2	Understanding	Try to learn some rules to deal with difficult situation			
3	Practice	Be able to apply English to deal with common Customer Service Problem			
Test and Comments	Total Score (1 point for each section)				
	Tutor Comments:				

Unit 6 Cross-border E-commerce Customer Service(I)

Task Fulfillment Report

Title			
Class		Name	Student ID
Task Fulfillment Report			

1. Present your task and your plan for it.
2. Present difficulties you came across on completing the task and your solutions.
3. Present what you have learnt through all this process.

Write a report with no less than 200 words.

Scoring Criteria (10-score range)		
Tutor comments:	Attitude	
	Task Amount	
Scoring Rules		

1. Timely finish all tasks.
2. Finish the tasks in reasonable way.
3. Reliable, coherent, logical and intelligible report.
4. Unfinished task will lead to 1 point deduction, and copy to 5 points deduction.

Keys

Exercise 1

1. 竞争优势　2. 转换率　3. 品牌知名度　4. 云计算　5. 人工智能　6. 回头客
7. 在线实时聊天　8. 加购后放弃

Exercise 2

1. gratitude   2. take the initiative to   3. involves   4. put yourself in their shoes

5. anticipated

Exercise 3

1. delayed

2. reputation

3. appreciation

4. impression

5. promoting

Exercise 4

1. request

2. supplier

3. agreement

4. unable

5. handle

6. recommend

7. unsatisfactory

Unit 7

Cross-border E-commerce Customer Service(Ⅱ)

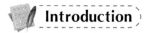

Introduction

Good customer service is kind of competitive advantage for companies. It tries to boost sales through resolving uncertainty before the deal, helps to elevate the purchasing experience of customers in order to promote products or the brand in a word-of-mouth way during the deal and solves the after-sales problems to lower the occurrence of dispute. For E-commerce, these functions are of great importance to promote the conversion rate and brand awareness. In this section, we are going to try to find some typical "scripts" in some common situations.

Contents

Part A Basic Online Communication Skills of Customer Services
Part B Practices of Customer Service for B2B
Part C Tips and Templates for Customer Service in Some B2C Scenarios

 Learning Aims

- Understand the rules of customer service in E-commerce.
- Observe practices for Cross-border E-commerce Customer Service.
- Learn tips to prepare customer for service scripts for both B2B and B2C.

 Capability Aims

- Be able to design the customer service procedure for an E-commerce.
- Be able to provide suitable response in some cases.
- Be able to prepare customer service scripts for possible situation.

Related Materials

Part A Basic Online Communication Skills of Customer Services

As we mentioned in the previous unit, online communication is the basic channel between customers and merchants chatting with shopping experiences and deal with all related problems. E-commerce communication is much more than a collection of words. The way you answer an E-mail or what you say on social media such as instant messenger does directly affect people's impression on you and the products you sell. As we all know, some of today's business relationships exist entirely online with the service provider and the client never meet face to face or never talk on the phone. Therefore, what are basic skills for bilateral online communication? The answers are in details as follows.

1. Make Sure Your Online Image Positive

Because we exchange so much information through websites, E-mails and social media, the way we conduct ourselves online is as important as how we appear in front of persons. Whereas an offhand spoken comment may be easily dismissed, anything you say online can be expanded and shared.

As a business owner, you should always ask yourself exactly what you intend to communicate before you share. You have to make sure that your communication is effective, consistent and builds confidence in customers' mind. To help guarantee your online business success, keep basic polite behavior is the first step.

2. Follow Grammar and Punctuation Rules

Speaking to make the communication effective, following basic grammar and punctuation rules is especially important. In any **virtual communication**, such as texting, blogging, or E-mailing, please remember to use real words, complete sentences and avoid **the signal of emoticons**. Sending a uniform and unambiguous message through all modes of communication is important. In words, you should write the way you were taught in school and avoid all but the most common **Internet abbreviations**. Please be careful about typing out the words without thinking and skip the ones that are inflammatory. And do never curse. How to compose a satisfied E-mail or message to the customer? We will talk about language skills of customer service in following parts.

3. Follow up with E-mail Communication

After a purchase or **cart trailing**, a follow-up E-mail can be very good for customer experience as well as securing repeat business. Please notify that a follow-up E-mail is not a purchase confirmation E-mail. In a follow-up E-mail, you ask for feedback on whether your customer is satisfied with the purchase and shopping experience. If customers are willing to write a review comment about the fact they purchased, you can offer them a coupon to be used on their next purchase. This method makes your customers feel that their business behavior is appreciated and that someone respects and cares about how they feel.

Sometimes a long E-mail is necessary, please be respectful by making it easy to read as possible and put the most important information at the top as well as organizing it in short paragraphs.

4. Pick up the Phone When Necessary

When a purchase is related to some necessary details or rules you need notify to customers seriously, please move it to the phone. At this moment, endless E-mail strings or text messages are frustrating and eventually create too much confusion.

5. Stay Neutral

When it comes to writing an E-mail, please <u>strive for</u> clear and matter-of-fact content. You can't go wrong if you remain as unbiased as possible in your online communication. Firstly, please take care choosing your professional user's name. If you own a business, having an E-mail address with your own domain name is necessary. Moreover, put some thought into identifiers for yourself that are easy for others to see. Going back to behavior, do not be funny, <u>sarcastic</u> or aggressive. It is probably best to avoid these <u>tactics</u> in oral exchange in the business world as well.

In all, these online communication strategies are positive for a successful E-commerce business and you will be sure to develop successful online business relationships.

Questions

Q1: In your words, can you summarize the tips to help you to build a satisfying online business relationship between customers and business owners?

New Words and Terms

1. bilateral	adj. 双边的,双方的
2. offhand	adj. 随意的,随便的
3. unambiguous	adj. 清楚的,不模糊的
4. inflammatory	adj. 煽动性的,使人发怒的

续表

5. sarcastic	adj. 讽刺的
6. tactic	n. 策略，解决方法
7. social media	社交媒体，社交软件
8. instant messenger	即时聊天工具（客服沟通时常用）
9. strive for	争取，谋求

Notes

1. virtual communication：虚拟社交；现代人的社交方式从以前的面对面真人社交转变为网络虚拟社交，尤其在聊天软件和网购平台风靡的今天，虚拟社交成为当代年轻人的主要生活方式。
2. the signal of emoticons：网络聊天表情符号，在 QQ 聊天和微信聊天软件上尤其流行，表情符号可以代替文字表达当时的心情和内心感受，在网购客服沟通交流中也经常使用。
3. Internet abbreviations：网络流行语缩写，在网络聊天和虚拟社交中常用，但不适用于电子商务贸易中的客服沟通。
4. cart trailing：购物车追踪；在电子商务贸易中，尤其是在客户服务中，客服会根据客户的购物车内容推送一些类似商品来判断客户的喜好，以便长期和客户保持良好的贸易关系，这类大数据分析和判断方法在网购平台上被频繁使用。

Part B Practices of Customer Service for B2B

The ways dealing with B2B and B2C customer service are somewhat different. They usually take to different tools to communicate. They usually happen in different scenarios and CS for B2B should contain some key information that may not be needed in B2C situation. In this section, we will talk about some CS practices for B2B.

The E-commerce platforms usually provide supportive system for sellers. For example, **Alibaba.com** provides their clients "My Alibaba", which is a very useful supportive system. You could also use your own CRM system to cope with these things. Let's talk about some pre-made scripts for some possible situations. Of course, you need customize them when actually do the work.

1. RFQ and Business Opportunities

Request for Quotation（RFQ）is an important channel for suppliers to get access to the information of their target market. B2B platforms, for example, Alibaba.com, provide this support. Once as a supplier, you find a potential customer through RFQ, you could check the information with the help of the platform.

Step 1: Check the information through RFQ research. When you find the potential client, check the information of that client and the number of quotations he has got. (picture 7-1; picture 7-2)

picture 7-1

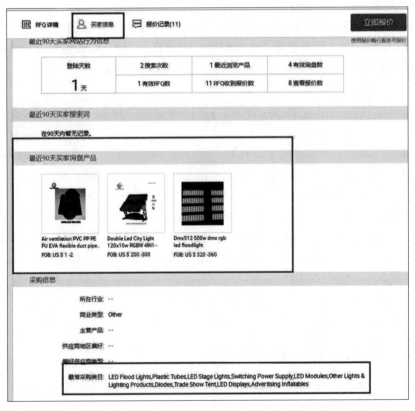

picture 7-2

Step 2: Find out the profile page of that client, try to figure out his preference and calculate the price you may offer. (picture 7-3)

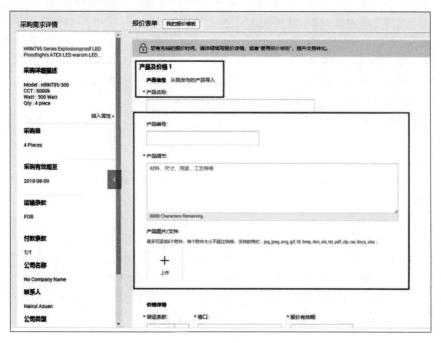

picture 7-3

Step 3: Send your quotation through the platform. It hasn't done yet. If you haven't got the reply. It is highly advisable to find out the client's E-mail box and try to contact him. (picture 7-4)

picture 7-4

Here are some <u>templates</u> you can refer to.

(1) If you haven't got any reply. (This happens, especially when the competition is fierce.)

You can send the E-mail or message to introduce your company and show willingness to cooperate.

> Dear Sirs/Madams,
>   We learned from Alibaba.com that you are in the market for women's <u>garments</u>.
>   We are ＊＊ Company, specialized in designing and manufacturing women's clothing. Here we attach a list of products we regularly produce. You could also visit our store on Alibaba.com. Should you be interested in any of our products, please let us know and we shall be very glad to give you our best quotations.
>   We look forward to receiving your inquiry soon.
>   Yours sincerely
>   (Your name)

You could also send your message in this way, if your quotation has reached to the potential buyer.

> Glad to contact you again!
>   It is regret that I haven't received any information from you. May I have your idea about the offer? We are glad to satisfy your need upon receipt of your replay.
>   If there is anything we can do for you, we shall be more than pleased to do so. Really hope we can build a good cooperation with you.

Also, you can ask the potential client about your products and commend there are other products available.

> Good day!
>   My quotation of ＊＊ you might have received. What do you think of it? Would you kindly advise your comments at your convenience?
>   If these products fail your expectation, would you please tell me your specific requirement or details? I will re-offer as soon as possible.
>   I am glad to serve at any time!

(2) For the regular customers, you could send mails to inform them of some promotion activities.

Here is an example.

> Dear X,
>   Christmas is coming, and there is a heavy demand for Christmas gifts. Here is our Christmas gifts link. If you are interested, please click to check them. All the products are now available from stock. Thank you for your attention.
>   Best regards.
>   (Your name)

2. Reply to Enquiry (Inquiry)

Usually, the buyer's enquiry contains questions about prices, sizes, specifications, quantity, payment, package, fulfillment, and they usually ask for catalogues, price lists, and samples. The reply to enquiry usually leads to the beginning of a deal. It is of great importance to have your reply done in a prompt, clear, polite and professional manner.

There are usually **general inquiry** and **specific inquiry**. You should pay attention to the requests in enquiry. When you try to reply the enquiry, you'd better convey the following information.

① You'd better repeat the date of the enquiry and express your appreciation.

② You should answer the questions in the enquiry and provide the things (catalogues, price lists) they ask for.

③ You could encourage (sometime push) the potential buyer to make the deal as soon as possible.

④ You'd better show your positive and energetic attitude.

Here are some examples.

(1) You can reply a general enquiry in this way.

Dear X,

Thank you for your inquiry of Aug.15.

We have these items in stock, our products are both excellent in quality and reasonable in price. Moreover, in August and September, we offer a 5% discount for **bulk purchase**.

Thank you again for your interest in our products. If you would like to have more information, please let us know. We look forward to your further reply.

Best regards.

(Your name)

---

(2) You can reply to a specific enquiry in this way.

Dear X,

Thank you for your inquiry of Aug. 15 and we are pleased to send you our quotation for the goods your required as follows:

Commodity: Women's Cocktail Summer Dress in assorted colors. Item No. UC-10001

Quantity: 100 dozen

> Size: Extra Large (XL) Large(L), Medium (M), Small(S), Extra Small (XS)
> (The specific size table is attached)
> Color: Pink   Light Blue   White   Black   Light Grey
> (The Color Board is attached)
> Price: at US$ 80 per dozen **CIF Honolulu**
> Shipment: in August, 2021
> Payment: by irrevocable L/C at sight
> **This offer is subject to our final confirmation.** If you find it acceptable, please let us have your reply as soon as possible.
> Your faithfully,
> (Your name)

(3) Bargaining occurs often, and you can reply it in this way.

> Dear X,
> Thank you for your letter of August 16. As regards your **counter-offer**, we regret we can't accept it because we feel that the price listed is reasonable and that leaves us limited profit already.
> However, in order to meet you on this occasion, we are prepared to grant you a special discount of 3% on condition that your order is not less than 1000 pieces.
> We hope to receive your order at an early date.
> Best regards,
> (Your name)

Tips: Here the terms and fulfillment methods are the same with other international trade. You can check more terms and methods for B2B according to international trade practices.

New Words and Terms

1. customize		v.（根据用户需求）修改，订制
2. template		n. 模板，样板
3. garment		n.（正式）服装
4. fulfillment		n. 履行，执行(任务)，在电商中常常指配送

Notes

1. Alibaba.com：阿里巴巴国际站是专业的国际外贸出口、海外 B2B 跨境贸易平台，主营

B2B(Business to Business)业务。

2. RFQ：Request for Quotation，阿里巴巴国际站称之为"采购直达"，这里的 quotation 指国际贸易中的"报价"。

3. general inquiry/specific inquiry：inquiry（也可用 enquiry）指国际贸易中的"询盘"；general inquiry 指"一般询盘"，specific inquiry 指"具体询盘"。

4. bulk purchase：批量购买，bulk 在贸易中一般理解为"大宗的"。

5. CIF Honolulu：CIF(Cost Insurance and Freight)是国际贸易术语，指货价包括成本、保险费和运费，这里的目的地是檀香山。

6. This offer is subject to our finally confirmation：There are Firm Offer(实盘) and Non-firm Offer(虚盘)。

When the Firm Offer is provided, it has legal effect. Once the Firm Offer is accepted, it is not subject to change at will and the supplier cannot withdraw it without the other party's consent. The offers containing the following expressions usually show that they are firm.

* The offer is subject to your acceptance reaching us not later than August 31.
* The offer remains firm (valid) until August 31.
* Our offer will remain valid for ten days.

However, the Non-firm Offer doesn't have legal bind on the supplier, and it is open to change. When you read the following expressions in the offer, you will find it should be a non-firm offer.

* The offer is subject to our final confirmation.
* The offer is subject to change without notice.
* We offer, subject to goods being unsold.

7. counter-offer：还价，还盘。

Exercises

Task 1：Role play：Suppose that you were doing business, and try to write an E-mail to a potential buyer to promote your products.

Task 2：Here is an inquiry letter. Please write a proper reply to it and offer your quotation.

From Westhouse Co.
4 Privet Drive, Little Whinging, Surrey
August 15, 2021
To the Manager Sales
Dear Sir/Madam,
　　We have read your information from Alibaba.com and are interested in it. We deal in various kinds of household utensils and crafts.

> We have recently started to stock and sell kitchenware and household porcelain and are sole agents of a couple of popular brands. We shall feel obliged if you send us your trade terms for ordering in bulk. We would also like to know if you can supply us your products on account if we provide you excellent bank and trade references.
> Yours Sincerely
> Cynthia

Part C Tips and Templates for Customer Service in Some B2C Scenarios

It shows that most online B2C sellers tend to use live chat support to communicate with their customers. It depends the rules and regulations, however. As we talked before, Amazon doesn't allow the direct contact between the seller and the buyer. Wish, too, does not offer such support. However, no matter through what kind of tool, it is still very practical and convenient to prepare customer for service scripts. In this part, we will talk about some possible situations and tips to create the script.

Before we assume the possible scenarios, let's get down to a basic rule. The Rule No.1: try to avoid the negative expressions.

For example, if you were the customer, when you hear "I can't get you that product until next month; it is back-ordered and unavailable at this time.", how do you feel?

How about saying that like this: "That product will actually be available next month. I can place the order for you right now and make sure that it is sent to you as soon as it reaches our warehouse!" And you can feel the difference.

Here are some possible situations as follows.

1. Different Scenarios in Need of Customer Service Support

1.1 Order Issues

Order issues can happen for many different reasons. Maybe there was a system error, or maybe the shopper accidentally purchased the wrong item or product variation. These are the possible situations:

1) The customer can't place order.
2) System placed order incorrectly.
3) Customer wants to change their order within the allowable time limit.
4) Customer wants to change their order outside of the allowable time limit.
5) There is no order confirmation email.

Here is a tip: A <u>helpdesk</u> for E-commerce will allow you to proceed to order create, duplicate, cancel and refund in one click directly from the ticketing system.

Let take one situation as an example.

> Situation: Customer wants to change their order within the allowable time limit
> Script:
> Your order (order-id) was within the past four hours, so I can cancel this order for you. You'll receive the cancellation <u>confirmation</u> in a few minutes by email, and you will be fully refunded. You can re-order what you'd like. Let me know if I can help you with anything else.

1.2 Shipping Issues

Shipping issues must be one of the most common issues the custom service agents may come across. The request may include:

1) Tracking shipment.
2) Late shipment.
3) Lost shipment.
4) Need to change shipping options after ordering.

Still, it is highly commended to use a customer helpdesk connected to your E-commerce platform, and you could insert customer <u>variables</u> like the last order id and tracking URL dynamically into your answer. Still, let's take an example.

> Situation: Lost shipment
> Script:
> We're sorry this order got lost in the mail. Would you like a replacement shipped to you or a full refund? If you'd like a replacement, we can offer 2-day shipping at no additional cost to you.

1.3 Product Problems

Sometimes the issue isn't technical or accidental. The issue just might be your product. Maybe the customer is disappointed by what they received. You can use these customer service scripts to reach resolution quickly and help potentially angry customers:

1) Product listing issues (not as described, pictured).
2) Negative product reviews.
3) Product questions.
4) Damaged products.
5) Product listing issues (not as described, pictured).

Situation: Negative product reviews
Script:

I understand you have concerns about some of the reviews you've seen. Our product isn't a fit for everyone, but we have 2000 positive reviews from customers who love it! There are no risks, as we offer a full refund if you ship the unused portion back to us within 30 days.

Situation: Damaged products
Script:

We're sorry that you received a damaged product. We try our best to make sure items reach you in perfect condition, but sometimes mistakes happen. Please send the item back to us using a prepaid label, which you can print here: (link).

We'll ship you a replacement right away.

1.4 Returns

Returns are also one of the most common E-commerce customer support issues. However, offering fast and easy returns is essential for growing your E-commerce business. We are proposing some possible situations, and you can prepare the scripts according to your routine.

1) Request to return product.
2) Request to return product outside of policy.
3) Tracking status of return.

Situations: Request to return product permitted by policy
Script:

Thanks for contacting us! We allow returns up to 30 days from the purchase date for all items except clearance items. You can initiate your return and print a shipping label with our easy return portal here: (link)

Situation: Request to return product outside of policy
Script:

Thank you for contacting us. Unfortunately, your order is outside of the window of return. However, because it is only outside the window by a couple days, I can allow you to return the item. Please confirm you'd still like to return it and I will email the prepaid shipping label. If we don't receive the product within 10 days, we will not be able to accept your return.

1.5 Billing and Payment

When there are payment issues, customers can easily become frustrated. Tread lightly and respond politely with these scripts for positive customer interactions. The possible situations may include:

1) Enquiry on accepted payment options.
2) Gift card not working.
3) Coupon code not working.
4) Stacking coupon codes.

Still, you can prepare the script with your company policy. Here follow examples.

> Situation: Enquiry on accepted payment options
> Script:
> Hi, thank you for contacting us. I'm happy to help with all of your questions. Regarding payment, we accept Visa, MasterCard, American Express, PayPal, and gift cards. Do you have any other questions?

> Situation: Stacking coupon codes
> Script:
> I'm sorry, but coupon codes can't be used together. Please choose one coupon code to use per order. Is there anything else I can help you with today?

Conclusion: For online sellers, to improve the efficiency of customer service, it is helpful to prepare some customer service scripts. They can help you systematize the way that you respond to customer inquiries and peed up response times, ensure quality customer service every time, and improve your support operations.

New Words and Terms

1. variation	n. 变体/更改的版本
2. helpdesk	n. 帮助台；超文本文档帮助信息
3. confirmation	n. 确认，证实
4. variable	n. 变量，可变因素
5. essential	adj. 极其重要的
6. routine	n. 常规；正常顺序
7. initiate	v. 发起；创始
8. stack	v. 堆叠，叠成一摞

Exercises

Task 3. Write another two live chat scripts of customer service for possible situations.

Task 4. Draw a flowchart (流程图) to guide customs to get a refund/replacement.

Learning Aims Achievement and Test

Section	Cross-border E-commerce Customer Service (Ⅱ)	Class hours		Course Credit	
Level	Medium	**Capability**	Capability to assist customers to accomplish their purchases	**Subtask**	4
Number	**Contents**	**Criteria**			**Score**
1	basic concept	Be able to tell the basic rule of customer service.			
2	Reply to inquiry	Be able to write a proper reply to inquiry or offer an attractive quotation.			
3	CS script writing	Be able to write polite and sound CS scripts.			
4	CS flowchart drawing	Be able to draw a clear flowchart to assist customer service.			
Test and Comments	Score (1 point for each section)				
	Tutor Comments:				

Task Fulfillment Report

Title	
Class	Name	Student ID	

Task Fulfillment Report

1. Present your tasks and your ideas about them.
2. Present difficulties you came across on completing the task and your solutions.
3. Present what you have learnt through all this process.

Write a report with no less than 200 words.

Scoring Criteria (10-score range)

| Tutor comments: | Attitude | |
| | Task Amount | |

Scoring Rules

1. Timely finish all tasks.
2. Finish the tasks in reasonable way.
3. Reliable, coherent, logical and intelligible report.
4. Unfinished task will lead to 1 point deduction, and copy to 5 points deduction.

Unit 8

Policies and Terms on Cross-border E-commerce Platform

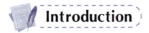 **Introduction**

Similar to other types of businesses, you need to comply with the general corporate laws and local and international laws applicable to your business when dealing with Cross-border E-commerce. However, it is said that 75% of Amazon sellers are worried about Amazon abruptly shutting down their account or listings which seems without any reason. (Jungle Scout) When you begin E-commerce, account suspensions could result in the loss of your massive investment of time, energy, and money. Everything you've spent on your business can vanish in an instant. The policies and terms systems of Cross-border E-commerce platforms are overwhelming and tricky. However, it is worthwhile to spend some time and energy looking into them. In this section, we are going to check some common pitfalls and try to avoid violations of policies.

Contents

    Part A   Various Policy and Common Pitfalls
    Part B   Intellectual Property
    Part C   Appeal and Plan of Action
    Supplementary Reading

 Learning Aims

- Understand the common terms about online E-commerce platform policies.
- Know some common pitfalls for sellers.
- Know some rudiments about IP.

 Capability Aims

- Be able to acquire information about policy and terms.
- Be able to apply the rules learned to operation plan.
- Be able to check operation procedures to avoid tricky situations caused by policy violation.

 **Related Materials**

Text A Various Policies and Common Pitfalls

Just as all other business, Cross-border E-commerce sellers should follow the code of ethics. It is extremely important to observe the local and the international laws and respect the local culture of the target market. However, there are also a lot of platform policies to follow. In the first two sections, we are going to look into some very common pitfalls which may lead to account suspension or even banned by the E-commerce platforms and thus to remind you to weigh before launching a new product.

1. The consequence of policy violation.

Let's talk the consequence first. Violation of laws usually led to lawsuit troubles. However, besides that, there are other account interruptions. We will take Amazon as an example and there are similar consequences with other platforms. There are usually 3 steps of action for Amazon.

1.1 Suspension

The first step Amazon takes when removing a seller's privileges from its platform is to suspend the seller's account. This may seem like bad news, but being suspended actually means that you have a chance to contest the suspension.

And, if you're lucky, Amazon will have revealed the reasons for the suspension in their notification, along with time frame to appeal — typically seven days.

Usually, when this happens, it means responding to Amazon's concerns by writing a **Plan of Action** letter detailing how you will address their issues with your account.

1.2 Denied

After you've submitted a Plan of Action to Amazon, your POA may get denied. A denied status isn't the end of the world though. You can rewrite and resubmit it to make your case.

Also, there is no set limit to the number of times that appeals can be resubmitted. There are claims on seller forums that say some sellers have submitted multiple appeal letters until they finally gave the POA Amazon was looking for. (This is unapproved by Amazon official channels.)

1.3 Banned

Finally, the worst-case-scenario for a suspended Amazon seller is a complete ban.

Once banned from the platform, Amazon will no longer read your emails or accept your Plans of Action. In other words, you're done.

It may be possible to start another account, but Amazon is pretty good about "sniffing out" dummy accounts, so a ban usually (and effectively) ends your career as an Amazon seller.

2. Tips for Cross-border Sellers to Prevent Account Suspension

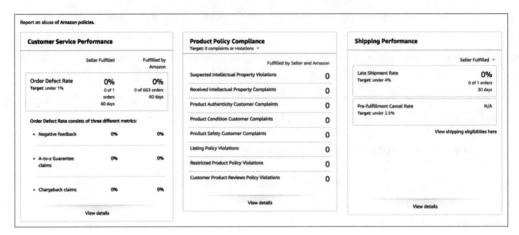

picture 8-1

Even there is no lawsuit trouble, these interruptions could incur heavy loss of buyers. For some sellers, some platforms, such as Amazon, seem to be very vague about the reason for account suspension. However, there are some useful guides to avoid having your selling privilege removed. First, let's begin with Amazon's *Account Health* and check the indicators for a healthy account. (See picture 8-1) Amazon sellers can check this in seller's center.

According to the criteria for a healthy account, it can be concluded that what Amazon values are the seller's customer service performance and compliance with the platform policy. From this perspective, 3 points can be drawn.

1) You should maintain a low **order defect rate** to keep the account healthy.

2) Sellers should watch the terms of policy closely.

3) There is requirement on shipping performance too. Sellers located in China should seriously consider the inventory plan, either leasing warehouse abroad or taking FBA terms.

In this part, we would like to talk about product policy compliance. Your products must not violate any of Amazon's product policies. A single complaint in any of the following categories can jeopardize your seller status:

* IP violations
* Product authenticity claims
* Listing policy violations

* Product condition claims
* Product safety claims
* Restricted product policy violations
* Customer product review policy violations

There are a lot of cases resulted from **IP violations**, listing policy violations and customer product review policy violations. However, as IP (intellectual property) is a very complicated problem, we will talk about it in Part B and there would be tips and warnings against inappropriate marketing activities in this part.

2.1 Check the Restricted Products Catalogue

Usually, there are long lists of restricted products for each platform. It is very important to check these lists before launching a new store on that platform. Also, it is reasonable to take a little time to get information about taboos of the countries where target markets are located. Don't sell any product related to that list. Usually, the following listed products are restricted on most Cross-border platforms:

1. Products with profanity
2. Words relating to sex or sexual activity
3. Product contains a drug image or text
4. Product pictures or description with the prejudice language or image
5. A product or image that shows a naked human body or sexual innuendo
6. Weapon.

> **Ratings, Feedback, and Reviews**
>
> You may not attempt to influence or inflate customers' ratings, feedback, and reviews. You may request feedback and reviews from your own customers in a neutral manner, but may not:
>
> - Pay for or offer an incentive (such as coupons or free products) in exchange for providing or removing feedback or reviews
> - Ask customers to write only positive reviews or ask them to remove or change a review
> - Solicit reviews only from customers who had a positive experience
> - Review your own products or a competitors' products

picture 8-2

2.2 Watch out Customer Product Review Policy Violations

Please pay attention to this point. Picture 8-2 is a screenshot from www.amazon.com. This piece of advice is very important for Chinese sellers. For years, as buyers in Taobao, we are accustomed to the inserted card with goods on which there is promise of cash or refund from the seller on condition that positive reviews were given. Such practice will be illegal in China very shortly.

However, for years, Amazon has worked diligently to create new processes and procedures to take care of its fake review issue. Of course, the biggest move it made was banning incentive reviews. Only recently did the word 'insert' appear in Amazon's terms of service language. Now, if a seller includes a product insert that specifically requests a positive review, or gives an incentive for a review, they can face review suppression and account suspension. However, it is said that Amazon isn't banning all product inserts though. We just have to make sure that the language in the insert is completely neutral. What is NOT allowed on product inserts is incentives for reviews.

Besides fake reviews and incentive reviews, sellers should also watch out the language. It should also be warned against using manipulative dialogue in messaging and promotional material.

Here are some examples of manipulative language:

Guilting the buyer. Saying you're a "small, family-owned business", that you're "donating to charity," or your products are "made in America" all qualify as guilting the buyer. Explaining that you donate profits to charity, you are "a family-owned business", or any other language that suggests not leaving a review could damage your business or hurt others.

Cherry-picking. "If there is any reason why you wouldn't leave a five-star review, please contact us." Even an image of five stars is problematic.

Incentivizing. Anything that induces positive behavior around reviews (discounts, unnecessary refunds, etc.).

Conflict of interest. Encouraging reviews from friends and family.

Amazon's tools can detect it. Amazon has suspended sellers for all of the above.

2.3 Selling Policy Violation

Many sellers want multiple business accounts because they are very deliberately breaking Amazon's Terms of Service and they are terrified of having their account shut down. By having multiple accounts they're able to hedge their bets. If one account gets shut down, they can simply start selling their products on the other account. This might not sound like such a big deal but it can have serious impact on your business as competitors are able to more liberally violate Amazon's selling policies.

However, from April 2020, Sellers with a legitimate business reason for multiple accounts no longer need Amazon's approval to open multiple accounts. Once you've exceeded a few hundred thousand dollars in revenue, it is not a bad idea to open a second Amazon Seller Central account.

Even though Amazon has stated that you do not need their approval to open a second account, it is still recommended that you open a case with them to request permission just to be safe. If Amazon gives you permission for a second account, they require the following: a separate bank account, separate email, and separate credit card. They do not require a separate business or personal entity.

In conclusion, from the stand point of the platform, it is extremely important to

Multiple Selling Accounts on Amazon

You may only maintain one Seller Central account for each region in which you sell unless you have a legitimate business need to open a second account and all of your accounts are in good standing. If any of your accounts are not in good standing, we may deactivate all of your selling accounts until all accounts are in good standing.

Examples of a legitimate business justification include:

- You own multiple brands and maintain separate businesses for each
- You manufacture products for two distinct and separate companies
- You are recruited for an Amazon program that requires separate accounts

picture 8-3

nurture an air of fair play. It is not commended to take those so-called black hat strategies.

New Words and Terms

1. comply with	遵守
2. account suspension	账户遭冻结
3. vanish	v. 消失
4. pitfall	n. 陷阱,隐患
5. violation	n.（对法律、协议的）违反
6. observe	v. 遵守
7. privilege	n. 权力
8. notification	n. 通知
9. time frame	时间范围,时间段
10. appeal	v. 申诉
11. dummy accounts	假账户
12. jeopardize	v. 危及,危害
13. restricted product	限售产品
14. profanity	n. 脏话,下流话
15. prejudice	n. 偏见
16. innuendo	n. 暗指;影射
17. diligently	adj. 勤奋的
18. manipulative	adj. 操纵的,会摆布人的
19. hedge	n/v. 防止损失（尤指金钱）的手段

Notes

1. plan of action (POA)：行动计划；当你的亚马逊账号因为系统问题而被暂停使用时，你需要写一封POA申诉信；在这封POA中，卖家需要对店铺做出有效、有策略的改变，以提高店铺运营效率；你的目标就是让亚马逊恢复你的账号和预防以后被亚马逊再次封号。
2. order defect rate (ODR)：不良体验订单率即买家不良体验订单占所有考核订单的比例；根据考核结果将卖家分为优秀、良好、及格和不及格卖家，不同等级的卖家将会获得不同的平台资源。
3. IP violation：Intellectual Property Violation，侵犯知识产权。
4. incentivized review：奖励性好评，"好评返现"就是一种典型的奖励性好评；fake review 是指请人刷单。

Exercise 1. Fill the blanks.

1. 跨境电商卖家应该遵守伦理道德规范，遵守当地和国际法律，尊重目的市场的文化。

Cross-border E-commerce sellers should _____ the code of ethics, _____ the local and the international laws and _____ the local culture of the target market.

2. 在发售新产品前，检查平台限售商品目录。

Check _____ on the platform before the launching of new products.

3. 亚马逊禁止刷单和奖励性评价。

Amazon bans _____ and _____.

4. 有些卖家希望利用多重账户对冲规避风险。

Some buyers hope to hedge the bet by having _____.

Task 1：Decide whether the following actions proper or not. Explain why it is proper or not.

1. Launch a new series of T-shirts with offensive sexism words.
2. Mark "We will donate 1% of the deal to charity." on the listing page.
3. Be prepared to sell obesity drug on Shopee.
4. Send an E-mail to the buyer, asking for positive review.
5. Insert a card with the product, promising a "red packet" of $1 with a positive review.
6. Ask your friends and relatives to make fake deals and give positive reviews.

Task 2：Search the restricted product list on AliExpress and another Cross-border E-commerce platform (for example Shopee). Draw two mind maps about them.

Text B Intellectual Property

Intellectual property (IP) refers to creations of the mind—inventions, literary and artistic works, and symbols, names, and images used in commerce. Under intellectual property law, owners are granted certain exclusive rights—intellectual property rights (IPR)—to the discoveries, inventions, words, phrases, symbols, and designs they create.

Trademarks, patents and copyrights are considered business intellectual property and, thus, protected by respective laws. According to **United States Patent and Trademark Office**, these terms can be defined in this way.

Trademark: A word, phrase, symbol and/or design that identifies and distinguishes the source of the goods of one party from those of others.

Patent: A limited duration property right relating to an invention, granted by the United States Patent and Trademark Office in exchange for public disclosure of the invention.

Copyright: Protects works of authorship, such as writings, music and works of art that has been tangibly expressed.

Before we move on, there is a very important fact with IP right. IP licensing permission granted by the owner of the intellectual property to another to use it according to agree terms and conditions, for a defined purpose, in a defined territory, and for an agreed period of time.

When you enter the business of cross border E-commerce, you have to be very careful. The customers you face are from all over the world. What you sell online must comply with the policy of the platform and the law of the market you focus. One of the most important thing E-commerce sellers must be careful is **infringement**. Some inappropriate infringement activities can lead to serious consequences, even can cause the bankruptcy of your business. Avoiding infringement is the priority job before E-commerce sellers start to list their products to E-commerce platform.

To avoid all these troubles, you need be careful with the following infringements:
1) Trademark infringement,
2) Patent infringement,
3) Copyright infringement,
4) Unauthorized infringement.

If you are going to do with Cross-border E-commerce, you need to check the list with:
1) The keyword in the title of your listing,
2) The image of your product,
3) The description of your product.

The following are the tips to avoid these infringements.

1. Trademark infringement

It means the copy of products of famous brand, or the use of similar brand name without authorization.

Famous trademark means good brand recognition, and it can boost the sales. If you are selling that on Amazon, and you are in fact hijacking other sellers' products. Generally, most sellers have registered their own trademark if they are doing business on Amazon. When you are hijacking other seller's listing, there is a great chance that you will receive a complaint of trademark infringement.

For a long-term business and the safety of your Amazon seller account, E-commerce sellers should try to avoid hijacking. You can register your own trademark. If you are selling with a famous trademark which does not belong to you or unauthorized, which means you are selling fake products. It can lead to serious consequences. When the amount you sold is big enough, you can be sentenced to prison for it.

2. Patent infringement

There are three types of patents:

1) **Utility patents** may be granted to anyone who invents or discovers any new and useful process, machine, article of manufacture, or composition of matter, or any new and useful improvement thereof;

2) **Design patents** may be granted to anyone who invents a new, original, and ornamental design for an article of manufacture; (This point should be highlighted. Design patent infringement is the most common issue in Cross-border E-commerce.)

3) Plant patents may be granted to anyone who invents or discovers and asexually reproduces any distinct and new variety of plant.

As E-commerce seller, you should inquire about your supplier if the products with patents or not. You can also check it in United States Patent and Trademark Office.

https://www.uspto.gov/patents-application-process/search-patents

(You can register your own trademark in United States Patent and Trademark Office.)

If there are some problems with the patent infringement of your products, do not hesitate: remove the listing immediately to make sure your seller account is safe. Otherwise, your seller account can be suspended once the infringements are compliant by others. Don't take the risk. It's not worthy.

3. Copyright infringement

It means to use the product photos, advertisements or product descriptions of others without authorization.

Copyright is a legal device that gives the creator of a literary, artistic, musical, or other creative work the sole right to publish and sell that work.

When E-commerce sellers are selling virtual products, such as PC Games, software and designs, you must be very careful. Do not commit copyright infringement. At the same time, if you are selling physical products, infringement of copyright always happens when sellers are using the pictures of the product provided by their suppliers. To avoid copyright infringement, try to take the pictures of the products by yourself.

4. Unauthorized infringement

It means to sell products without authorization. When sellers are authorized to sell products with famous brands, they can sell it on Amazon or other platforms with concern about the infringement. Make sure you are authorized before you start to sell branded products.

Commit any of these infringements and you may get involved in intellectual property claim. Intellectual property claims are legal actions brought by one party against another when a party feels its intellectual property (IP) rights have been infringed upon. Because many companies consider their IP to be their most valuable asset, they can often move aggressively to protect it if they feel an infringement has occurred. It is highly commended to handle IP issues in a very careful and discreet manner.

New Words and Terms

1. exclusive	adj. 专有的，独有的
2. disclosure	n. 发布，公开
3. tangibly	adv. 确凿地
4. territory	n. 领域，地区

Notes

1. United States Patent and Trademark Office：美国专利及商标局，是美国商务部下的一个机构，主要负责为发明家及其相关发明提供专利保护、商品商标注册和知识产权证明。
2. trademark：商标，指产品的制造商或销售商用来表示产品来源，将其与他人的产品相区别的文字或图形标志。
3. patent：专利（权），指就一项发明创造而由国家授予的一定期限的垄断权。
4. utility patent：发明专利，是指任何新且有用的程序、机器、制造或物质的组成，或者是上述任何新且有用的改进。
5. design patent：外观设计专利，是指对产品整体或者局部的形状、图案或者其结合以及色彩与形状、图案的结合所做出的富有美感并适用于工业应用的新设计。
6. infringement：侵权，常指对著作权、专利权、商标权、外观设计权等的侵害。

Exercise 2: Translate the following terms.

1. intellectual property right: _____
2. intellectual property claim: _____
3. 注册商标: _____
4. 侵犯版权的行为: _____
5. 未授权的侵权: _____

Task 3: Write a case research report about Design Patent infringement.

Text C　Appeal and Plan of Action

Sometimes, online sellers make mistakes for their negligence with the supply sources, and some would receive quite a few claims or refund requests for shipping or package conditions. All of these would lead to some actions taken by the platform. Different E-commerce platforms take different measures for violation. AliExpress and Alibaba.com have an accumulated points system. Each violation or poor performance leads to point minus. (According to the seriousness of that violation). Amazon would suspend, or ban the seller's account, as talked previously.

Having the seller's account suspended is not the end of the world, for you still have chance to appeal and amend. In this section, let's talk some tips about what to do after the Amazon seller's account getting suspended.

September 5, 2017
Your Amazon.com selling privileges have been removed

Sent from: seller-performance-policy@amazon.com

Hello,

You have not sent us an acceptable plan to address the complaints we received about your items. As a result, you may no longer sell on Amazon.com. Your listings have been removed from our site, and we are withholding any funds available in your account. If you have FBA inventory of the items that caused "inauthentic" complaints, they are currently ineligible for removal.

If you do not appeal this decision in 90 days, we will permanently withhold any payments to you, and any FBA inventory of the items that caused "inauthentic" complaints will be destroyed at your expense.

To appeal this decision, click the Appeal button next to this message on the Performance Notifications page in Seller Central (https://sellercentral.amazon.com/gp/customer-experience/perf-notifications.html).

The sale of counterfeit products on Amazon is strictly prohibited. If you cannot provide valid invoices or receipts for the items that caused "inauthentic" complaints, funds will be withheld equivalent to the amount you earned from the sale of these items in the last 180 days. If the equivalent amount is greater than the total amount available in your account, then the total amount will be held. If you have FBA inventory of these items, they will be destroyed at your expense.

Learn more about this policy in Seller Central Help
(https://sellercentral.amazon.com/gp/help/201165970).

You can see your balance and settlement information in the Payments section of Seller Central. If you have questions about those, please write to payments-funds@amazon.com.

Sincerely,

Seller Performance Team
Amazon.com
http://www.amazon.com

picture 8-4

Picture 8-4 is about an account suspension notification issued by Amazon. No seller would be happy to receive such notification. However, before preparing your appeal letter or Plan of Action, you should calm down and think about the whole thing.

Without a thoughtful plan of action (POA), you could waste your appeal button. Amazon rarely <u>reinstates</u> an account after the first appeal is sent. Unless it's a very minor violation, the process can take days, or even weeks and requires back and forth communication with Seller Performance.

If you just got the suspension notice from Amazon, make sure you do not respond until you take the following steps:

1) Determine exactly why Amazon decided to suspend your account.

2) Take steps to resolve the issues in the eyes of Amazon and the affected customers, if <u>applicable</u>.

3) Implement new systems to ensure the issues do not happen again.

If you are well prepared for the steps above, then you need to create a Plan of Action and <u>submit</u> it to Amazon. Although the requirements for your Plan of Action letter depend on what you did to get suspended/denied, here are the basics of what you should include:

1) Address the problem.

This may take some guess work as Amazon can be a little unclear regarding the reasons for any Amazon account suspensions. But, if you've done your due diligence and considered all of the things that could have caused the suspension/denial, pick the one that's most likely and highlight it.

For example, "I sold a product that was related to <u>marijuana</u>, which is a restricted product on Amazon."

2) Explain the actions you've taken to fix the problem. Next, explain to Amazon what you've done that fixes the issue at hand. These things should be done before you send your Plan of Action letter. In that way, you can submit evidence of the corrections you've made, along with your letter.

3) Explain how you plan to prevent future instances of the problem. Finally, describe to Amazon how you will avoid repeating the issue in the future — this is the actual "Plan of Action." This, more than any other action you take, is what Amazon wants to see.

They want to ensure that you understand the <u>severity</u> of the situation and that you're taking the proper steps to correct your mistakes. Always assume total ownership of the problem, even if you feel you were wrongly accused.

Often, POAs allow for <u>attachments</u>, so be sure to include any <u>receipts</u>, copies of email, <u>screenshots</u>, and any other proof that will help build your case for reinstatement.

However, there is still a chance that Amazon will deny your Plan of Action. If they do, read the denial letter carefully to see if there are any clues as to why it was denied. Then, address those issues one by one. In a word, you'd better try very hard whatever you can do to increase the odds you get your account back.

New Words and Terms

1. negligence	n. 疏忽，失误
2. reinstate	v. 使…复原
3. applicable	adj. 适用的，合适的
4. submit	v. 提交
5. marijuana	n. 大麻
6. severity	n. 严格
7. attachment	n.（电子邮件）的附件
8. receipt	n. 收据
9. screenshot	n. 屏幕截图

Task 4: Write a letter of POA based on the notification of picture **8-4**.

Supplementary Reading

How to Deal with Amazon A-to-Z Claims

In the event a customer purchases an item from a third-party seller and something goes wrong (for example, it fails to deliver on-time), the Amazon A-to-Z Guarantee is in place to protect customers (and their wallets).

What is the Amazon A-to-Z Guarantee?

Amazon's A-to-Z Guarantee covers two things - the timely delivery of your item and the condition of the purchased items.

If either is unsatisfactory, customers can report the problem to Amazon and their team will determine if the customer is eligible for a refund. This policy was put in place to protect the customers Amazon values.

Unfortunately, for sellers — too many A-to-Z claims (just like negative reviews) can severely damage the quality of the seller account and have a negative impact on the ability to sell.

As a seller, if you are hit with an A-to-Z claim, you should not take it lightly. Although it's not necessarily a death notice, if a seller acquires too many of these red flags, Amazon could suspend or terminate the account.

Why Does a Customer File an Amazon A-to-Z Claim?

Customers can file an A-to-Z claim provided they with first contact the seller and wait two days to give the seller an opportunity to resolve the problem.

This gives the customer and the seller a bit of time to resolve the issue on their own before Amazon will step in.

A customer can file an A-to-Z Claim if they meet one (or more) of the reasons below:

- The seller failed to deliver the item by 3 calendar days past the maximum estimated delivery date or 30 days from the order date, whichever is sooner.

- The item received was damaged, defective, materially different, or the customer changed their mind and returned it in line with Amazon's return policy but the customer has not been refunded or the refunded was in the wrong amount.

- The customer was not satisfied with the quality of the eligible services performed by the third-party seller.

- The customer wants to return an item internationally and the seller does not (1) provide a return address within the US, (2) provide a pre-paid return label, or (3) offer a full refund without requesting the item to be returned.

- The customer has been charged extra (for example, by customs authorities for shipment to US) in addition to the purchase and dispatch price they paid, and the seller did not cover those costs.

How a Customer Files an A-to-Z Guarantee Refund

To request a refund on an eligible order, the customer must follow the stipulated steps and the refund request(s) can take up to one week for Amazon to investigate.

Customers have up to 90 days after the maximum estimated delivery date to request a refund under the A-to-Z Guarantee.

Keep in mind: The A-to-Z Guarantee does not cover digital items, payments for services, stored value instruments. Additionally, if a customer files a chargeback with their payment provider or bank, they will not be eligible for a refund under the A-to-Z Guarantee.

How can Sellers Prevent A-to-Z Claims?

Although there's no surefire way to prevent A-to-Z claims, there are a number of preventative steps sellers can take to better their chances of a positive customer experience.

For example, at CPC Strategy we do not implement any advertising tactics until we have written or verbal approval from the clients who we work with that they are ready and able to properly accept, fulfill, and service orders within Amazon's seller performance thresholds.

The reason for this approach is to set up our clients for long term success and avoid any risks of suspensions, negative reviews, or A-to-Z claims which will damage the quality of the account and impact their ability to sell.

What if a customer is trying to "game the system" with returns? How can sellers protect themselves?

In some cases, customers will try to "game the system" with returns. But what does this mean exactly? And how can sellers better protect themselves in the event this happens?

Let's apply this to an example:

Company A sells inflatable kayaks through FBA. One of their biggest pain points is what they call the "triple hit" fee.

Fee 1: They have to pay shipping fees when a customer returns a product.

Fee 2: They also have to pay the FBA Weight Handling fee for the initial delivery & return shipping back to FBA Fulfillment Center.

Fee 3: And finally, they have to pay to ship the "unsellable" boards back to their own warehouse.

"This is especially frustrating when a customer appears to be 'gaming the Amazon system' by using the product for as long as they need it, say for a vacation, then returning it claiming it as defective."

— Joe Selzer Manager, Production & Integrations at CPC Strategy

So - is there a way for Company A to protect themselves from customers that attempt to take advantage of Amazon's return policy?

According to experts, unfortunately the seller doesn't have much control in these instances due to Amazon's customer friendly return terms.

The way FBA returns operation is that if the returned product is received in sellable condition, it will be returned to the original seller's inventory. If the returned product is received in a condition that the product cannot be resold, Amazon will determine who is at fault (Amazon or customer) and reimburse according to the FBA Lost and Damaged Inventory Reimbursement Policy.

"One of the things they'll need to balance here is the risk of inducing negative customer feedback and A-to-Z claims as a result of what is perceived to be poor customer service."

Reflection: Think of A-to-Z policy from both perspective of buyers and sellers.

Learning Aims Achievement and Test

Section	Policies and Terms on Cross-border E-commerce Platform	Class hours		Course Credit	

续表

Level	Medium	Capability	Capability to understand basics about the various policies and terms on Cross-border E-commerce platforms	Subtask	4
Number	**Contents**		**Criteria**		**Score**
1	Language skills		Understanding the terms of policies. Finish the Exercises in the texts.		
2	Basic Concept		Be able to find out the common improper acts in Cross-border E-commerce		
3	Capability to apply what have learnt		Be able to conduct some case research and complete the report.		
4	Capability to write practical writing		Be able to write a letter of POA with given information. (or would be voluntarily find some proofs to support POA)		
Test and Comments	Score (1 point for each section)				
	Tutor Comments:				

Task Fulfillment Report

Title				
Class		Name		Student ID
Task Fulfillment Report				

1. Present your tasks and your ideas about them.
2. Present the difficulties you came across on completing the task and your solutions.
3. Present what you have learnt through all this process.

Write a report with no less than 200 words.

	Scoring Criteria (10-score range)	
Tutor comments:	Attitude	
	Task Amount	
Scoring Rules		

1. Timely finish all tasks.
2. Finish the tasks in reasonable way.
3. Reliable, coherent, logical and intelligible report.
4. Unfinished task will lead to 1 point deduction, and copy to 5 points deduction.

Keys

Exercise 1:

1. follow, observe, respect   2. restricted products list
3. fake reviews, incentivize reviews

4. multiple business account

Task 1: All improper.

Exercise 2:

1. 知识产权　2. 知识产权请求权　3. register trademark

4. copyright infringement　5. unauthorized infringement

Unit 9

Cross-border E-commerce Online Payment

Introduction

Electronic payment is very convenient for customers in Cross-border E-commerce payment. To avoid writing up a check, swiping a credit card or handling paper money, more and more customers are turning to make use of **electronic payment**. Thus, electronic payment has become the most common method of payment for consumers in China.

Contents

Part A   An Introduction to Dominant Online Platforms Worldwide
Part B   Online Payment Platforms in China
Supplementary Reading

Learning Aims

- Learn different methods and platforms of payment worldwide
- Learn dominant platforms of online payment in China

Capability Aims

- Be able to understand popular international E-commerce online payment platforms.
- Be able to know how to use popular international online payment methods.
- Be able to identify the process of online shopping on websites and to know how to use international Alipay.
- Be able to identify and understand security problems and solutions of E-commerce online payment.

Related Materials

Text A An introduction to Dominant Online Payment Platforms Worldwide

It is acknowledged that electronic payment has become the most common method for customers in China. Therefore, in this article, we will browse dominant types of electronic payment for purchasers, which is commonly called customer payment platforms.

1. Customer Payment Platforms

Customer payment platforms are also named as the ways of customer payment. The capital turnover process from buyers to vendors is similar to the process of online-shopping in **Taobao**. One international customer purchased and the payment for goods will be transferred into the **third-party payment platform**. Then vendor will send out the products and after the buyer confirms the delivery, the third-party platform will transfer the money to the vendor's account. That is to say, it is a **one-time customer-to-vendor payment** which is commonly used when you shop online at an E-commerce site.

Of Cross-border E-commerce trade in China, making settlement is going through **international Alipay** which is a common way by swiping a credit card and international Alipay does accept almost all types of payment. It includes almost all cards printed with **VISA, UnionPay, MasterCard**, etc. International Alipay account is a product produced in Alipay China Network Technology Co., Ltd.

Unlike domestic Alipay account, this international Alipay account is a **multi-currency account, including USD and RMB accounts**. The third-party payment service of international Alipay is provided by the joint support of Alibaba international station and domestic Alipay. If you own any domestic Alipay account, you do not need apply for another international Alipay account. The only thing you should do is to bind the domestic Alipay account on E-commerce platform and you can collect transactions. Now international Alipay accepts four main types of payment as follows.

(1) Credit Card Payment

The buyer can pay for orders within VISA, MasterCard or **Maestro**. After complement of bills payment, if the vendor receives RMB, International Alipay will pay the order according to the exchange rate of the buyer on the day of payment. Please notice that the **exchange rate is determined by the bank and the exchange rate on the settlement date is generally two working days after payment**. If RMB is not wanted, International Alipay will transfer USD to the vendor.

(2) Debit Card Payment

The appearance of internationally accepted **debit cards** looks similar like credit cards, and the logo of the international payment card organization is printed in the lower right corner. When you use a debit card, the difference is that the debit card does not have credit line so that you only use the balance of the account for payment. i. e., Maestro Card is a type of debt card and it is supported by Alipay.

(3) T/T Bank Remittance and Western Union Remittance Payment

Bank remittances are still the mainstream payment method in international trade in large transactions. When the buyer uses this method for payment, the platform will settle the order payment into RMB and pay it to the buyer according to the exchange rate of the buyer on the day of payment. This method of remittance will charge some extra transfer fees and bank withdrawal will also produce a certain withdrawal fee.

(4) Moneybookers Payment

Moneybookers platform allows more than fifty types of worldwide payment, including all kinds of credit cards and debit cards. i.e., **AliExpress** opens a **"fast payment channel"** for more than ten multiple types of debit cards such as Maestro and **Post Pay**. When the buyer uses this fast payment channel for paying, the vendor will check "the debit card payment success" in order management.

2. Advantages of International Alipay

In China, Alipay is most widespread E-commerce payment for consumers. International Alipay has a lot of advantages. First of all, Alipay is not just a tool of payment but a third-party online payment service. After the capital comes to the buyer's Alipay account, the vendor will send out the products. This method makes the safety of the trade. In other words, Alipay will notify the vendor for goods delivery after getting the pay from the buyer to avoid any **fraud transaction** in payment process. Second, international Alipay is more convenient for instant payment and the withdrawal from Alipay needs no other extra application. When you apply for a withdrawal of money transaction, Alipay will transfer the money to your Alipay online account. Last but not least, Alibaba and Alipay both support international Alipay method which is potential development in the future.

3. Withdrawal of Sellers

It is acknowledged that the buyer pays for orders and the seller delivers the goods. After the buyer confirms the delivery, the payment will be remitted to the seller's Alipay account through the international Alipay platform. The seller withdraws cash in the form of balance withdrawal and the withdrawal is separated into USD withdrawal and RMB withdrawal. Withdrawal in USD will be sent to the user's USD bank account as well as withdrawal in RMB being sent to the user's RMB bank account.

Please notice that at the beginning the user needs set up a withdrawal account in RMB and in USD. After the account gets approval from Alipay, it makes withdrawal successful. Moreover, **withdrawal of USD requires at least 16 dollars per time and it charges extra 15 dollars fee each time. Withdrawal of RMB requires at least 10 cents per time and no extra fee is needed.**

Questions

1. Why more and more people are turning to electronic payment?
2. What do types of electronic payment include?
3. What are benefits of international Alipay?

New Words and Terms

1. convenient	adj. 方便的,便捷的
2. cheque	n. 支票
3. payment	n. 支付,付款
4. withdrawal	n. 提现
5. account	n. 账户
6. process	n. 资金周转流程
7. order	n. 订单
8. settlement	n. 结算
9. type	n. 种类
10. balance	n. 余额
11. transfer	n. 转账
12. delivery	n. 发货
13. electronic payment	电子支付
14. international settlement	国际结算
15. credit card	信用卡
16. paper money	纸币
17. exchange rate	汇率
18. payment for goods	货款
19. bank remittance	银行汇款
20. management system	管理系统
21. multicurrency species	多币种

续表

22. debit card	借记卡
23. pay off	付清钱款
24. payment service	支付服务
25. tools of payment	支付工具

Notes

1. electronic payment：电子支付，又名移动支付，是当下亚洲市场跨境电商贸易的普遍方法。

2. Taobao：中国的购物网站，同时也是亚太地区较大的网络零售商圈；淘宝网由阿里巴巴集团在 2003 年 5 月创立，是国内深受欢迎的网购零售平台，拥有近 5 亿的注册用户数，每天有超过 6000 万的固定访客，同时每天的在线商品数已经超过 8 亿件，平均每分钟售出 4.8 万件商品。

3. third-party payment platform：第三方支付平台；国内的电商贸易、商户对商户、个人对商户都普遍使用第三方平台支付费用，买家先支付费用到第三方平台，平台代为保管支付费用，待买家收到货物并确认无误以后，货款会由第三方平台转入卖方的账户。国内最大的第三方支付平台是支付宝。

4. one time customer-to-vendor payment：买卖双方一次性付款结算，强调一次付清，而非分期付款。

5. international Alipay：国际支付宝，与支付宝不同，国际支付宝仅在使用国际性网站购物时才会使用，例如速卖通网站、东南亚市场的 Lazada 网站；在这些网站购物时都会使用国际支付宝作为第三方支付平台。

6. VISA，UnionPay，MasterCard：比较普及的国际电子支付方式，通常这三个标志会印制在相应的银行卡右下方；VISA 是维萨信用卡，MasterCard 是万事达信用卡，UnionPay 是中国银联卡。

7. multi-currency account：多币种账户，国际支付宝就是多币种账户，分为美元账户和人民币账户。

8. Maestro：Maestro 是 MasterCard 其中的一个商标，Maestro 信用卡也是其下的信用卡之一。

9. exchange rate is determined by the bank and the exchange rate on the settlement date is generally two working days after payment：国际支付宝结算汇率是按照买家付款当天的汇率结算成人民币支付给卖家的。这里需要注意的是，汇率由收单银行确定，汇率清算日的汇率并非支付日，一般是支付后的 2 个工作日。

10. debit cards：借记卡是指持卡人先存款后使用的卡。国际通行的借记卡的外观与信用卡一样，其右下角印有国际支付卡机构的标志。

11. Bank remittance：银行汇款；银行汇款在大额交易时仍然是国际贸易的主流支付方

式,买家使用此方式支付,平台将会将订单款项按照买家付款当天的汇率结算成人民币支付给买家;这种汇款方式会产生转账手续费,提现也会产生一定的提现手续费。

12. AliExpress:这是前面注解里提到的速卖通平台。

13. fast payment channel:速卖通平台为多种借记卡在 Moneybookers 上开通了快速付款通道,买家可以直接使用快速付款通道支付货款。

14. Post Pay:贝宝。与 Paypal 国际支付结算不同的是,Paypal 支持多币种支付结算,贝宝只支持人民币交易服务。

15. fraud transaction:交易欺诈;电子支付最需要注意的是诈骗行为;国际支付宝是一种第三方支付服务,卖家先收款后发货,全面保障卖家的交易安全;当支付宝收到了买家的货款,才通知卖家发货,这样可以避免卖家使用其他支付方式时遇到交易欺诈。

16. withdrawal of USD requires at least 16 dollars per time and it charges extra 15 dollars fee each time. Withdrawal of RMB requires at least 10 cents per time and no extra fee is needed. 在国际支付宝账户中,用户需要先设置美元和人民币提现账户,设置完成后才能提现;需要注意的是,美元提现金额至少为 16 美元,人民币提现金额至少为 0.01 元,人民币提现无手续费,美元提现每次收取 15 美元的手续费。

Text B   Online Payment Platforms in China

Chinese customers pay for their purchases through a single transaction via other marketplace checkout system during searching for foreign products and comparing prices on various platforms. Although available credit cards are unpopular payment methods for Chinese e-consumers, they usually choose to pay via third-party online payment such as Alipay.

Chinese online payment platforms work similar to Western platforms such as **PayPal**. Customers' accounts are linked to their corporate online payment accounts. While different from instant cash transferring, Chinese online consumers typically prefer to pay through **escrow payments**, which they consider it to be safer. A customer's payment is put in an escrow account hosted by one of the third-party payment platforms after product ordering. Once the buyer receives the order and confirms the delivery on the online payment platform, the online payment platform will release the payment to the merchants.

Particularly in China, great importance has been attached to mobile payment. **Mobile phone payment service** always enables users to check account balances, transfer money, pay bills and conduct financial management anytime in anywhere. This service provides great convenience for users. **Alibaba**, which has been leading E-commerce companies in China, has started its mobile payment solution—Alipay. **Tencent**, a leading social network service provider, has developed **WeChat Pay**. **China Mobile**, which is another telecommunication service provider in China, has also offered mobile payment services such as enabling users to pay the bus fare with their mobile phones.

There is a number of payment options available, but none of them is equally effective in all regions worldwide. Credit cards are accepted worldwide, but while they have dominated the US and other Western E-commerce markets, they have not shown the same dominance in emerging markets in China and Asia. In these markets, merchants need to support other payment options.

Questions
1. What are two major online payment platforms in China?
2. What services do mobile phone payment service support?

New Words and Terms

1. Alipay	n. 支付宝
2. WeChat	n. 微信
3. checkout system	结算系统
4. third-party online payment	第三方支付
5. cash transfer	现金转账
6. escrow payments	支付代管
7. product ordering	商品下单
8. confirm the delivery	确认收货
9. release the payment	放款
10. mobile payment	手机支付;移动支付
11. WeChat pay	微信支付
12. telecommunication service	远程网络服务
13. bus fare	公交车票
14. emerging markets	新兴市场

Notes

1. PayPal：20 世纪 80 年代由一家美国公司创立的国际在线支付服务平台，支持 20 多个币种的在线支付服务。
2. escrow payments：支付代管，通常在第三方交易平台进行。在买家网购下单以后，买家通过第三方平台使用代管支付；待买家收到快递并使用在线支付平台确认收货以后，在线支付平台便会放款给商户。
3. mobile phone payment service：手机支付服务；移动支付现在已经成为中国国民生活的重要组成部分，移动支付除了可以实时支付日常花销以外，还支持随时随地检查账户余额、转账和理财等其他功能。

4. Alibaba：阿里巴巴集团控股有限公司，于1999年创立，创始人是马云，是一个电子商务综合运营集团，国内的淘宝网、支付宝、盒马生鲜等都隶属于此公司。

5. Tencent：腾讯集团，创立于1998年，是一家互联网公司，聊天软件腾讯QQ就是腾讯集团的第一款著名产品；腾讯集团现在依然致力于开拓互联网数字化产品，旗下开发并运营的腾讯视频是现在数字化流媒体平台上的一个范例。

6. WeChat Pay：微信支付；微信是腾讯集团开发的即时聊天社交工具，由此应运而生的微信支付也是腾讯公司的产物，现在的微信支付与支付宝已经成为国内移动支付的两大支柱平台。

7. China Mobile：中国移动通信；中国移动通信集团公司是中国规模最大的移动通信运营商，主要经营移动电话通话、数据、IP电话和多媒体业务，并支持计算机互联网上网功能。前面提到的微信支付和支付宝平台服务都需要网络的支持，而普遍和中国移动提供的网络数据服务叠加可以让用户的体验更好。

Supplementary Reading

Security Tips of Online Payments

E-commerce allows consumers to shop for almost anything from almost anywhere. But in terms of payment, E-commerce is as challenging as ever. Payment and fraud go hand in hand. For customers, when you make a purchase from your online store, can you protect your credit card information? If not, why would they continue to support your business? That's why protecting the customers' payment data should always be a priority. There are some tips for security of payment.

1. Do not Store Customer Payment Data

There are strict standards in place regarding the customer payment data that you store. If you do need to store information, such as a customer's name and account number, then take measures to protect this information like using a private network, or cloud-based storage or encrypting the data so that intruders cannot read it.

In addition, you are not allowed to include the full credit card number and expiration date of your customer's credit when e-mailing them the receipt. You are only permitted to display the last five numbers.

2. Choose a Secure E-commerce Platform and Processor

Despite the regulations that have been put in place, not all E-commerce platforms and processors take security as seriously as others. When looking for an E-commerce platform or processor, please choose trusted and reputable companies that have good reviews.

3. Verify the Transaction

There are several ways that you can do to verify the transaction. These tips include as follows.

Firstly, please always make sure that there is an address verification service in place and the web address verified and please require customers to enter their card security code where three-digit or four-digit card verification value is on the back of their cards.

Secondly, please be suspicious of some patterns, such as an exceptionally large order from a returning customer. If so, call the customer immediately and please review smaller details like strange e-mail address, products being shipped to areas known for instances of fraud, and customers not taking advantage of deals like free shipping. Considering accepting e-checks, payments from bank accounts have to be verified through the automated clearing house network.

4. Keep Your IT Environment Protected

Even if you have taken security precautions like having an SSL certificate on your website, you are still not completely free from problems. Having a firewall solution can help decrease these threats. A firewall is a hardware or software system that essentially works as a wall or gateway between two or more networks, permitting authorized traffic and blocking unauthorized traffic from accessing a network or system.

5. Update All of Your Systems

It's no secret that outdated systems do attract cyber attacks. You need to make sure that when there is a new update, it is downloaded immediately. Typically, these updated occur automatically, but it is always best to be on the side of caution by making sure that you are running the latest version of any software that you use for your business.

Above all, for merchants, standing on top of all these security measures can effectively build your customers trust, which contributes to the success of your business.

Notes

SSL certificate：SSL 服务证书协议；在网站上登录时会在验证服务器身份后颁发，具有服务器身份验证和数据传输加密功能；该安全协议主要提供对用户和服务器的认证；对传送的数据进行加密和隐藏，以确保网站用户的隐私信息安全；SSL 协议可以实现数据信息在客户端和服务器之间的加密传输，可以防止数据信息的泄露，保证了双方传递信息的安全性，而且用户可以通过服务器证书验证其访问的网站是否真实可靠。

Exercises

Task 1：Please research a newly-developed payment method and fill in the table with the information you get. Discuss online payment trends with your partner.

Payment Method	Provider	Features

Task 2: Please work in groups and discuss strengths and weaknesses of mobile phone payment, credit card payment, debit card payment and cash payment. You can list pros and cons of them in the following tables.

	Mobile Payment	Credit Card Payment	Debit Card Payment	Cash Payment
Pros				
Cons				

Task 3: Do a mini debate about the topic: "Is it possible that mobile phone payment could completely take the place of traditional ways of payment such as paying in cash?" Please list out your position and your reasons.

Exercises 1: Please match these pictures with correct Chinese names.

VISA	贝宝
ESCROW	维萨信用卡
WeChat Pay	银联支付
UnionPay International	西联国际汇款
MasterCard	微信支付
WESTERN UNION	第三方托管
PayPal	万事达信用卡

Exercises 2: Please translate the following words and phrases into English.

1. 账户
2. 余额
3. 订单
4. 结算
5. 提现
6. 电子支付
7. 移动支付
8. 第三方支付平台
9. 下单
10. 确认收货

Exercises 3: Please use the text information to complete the following sentences.

1. Online payment is generally going through _____, such as Alipay, PayPal, etc.

2. Name two international third party payment platforms: _____ and _____.

3. International Alipay account is a multi-currency account, which includes _____ account and _____ account.

4. Credit cards have credit _____ but debt cards do not own it.

5. One of the most common features about Alipay is that international Alipay is a _____ online payment platform.

Exercises 4: Please number the following online payment steps in right orders.

( ) Confirm delivery

( ) Order placement and payment in RMB in escrow

( ) Release escrow payment to Cross-border E-commerce platform

( ) Delivery of goods

( ) Share details order and logistics to overseas business

( ) Release escrow payment to merchants in other currency

Exercises 5: Extension task — You can make a speech within 6 minutes according to text B and you can choose the topic by yourself. If possible, make a short video of your speech.

Learning Aims Achievement and Test

Section	Study on international and domestic E-commerce Online Payment Platforms	Class Hours		Course Credit	
Level	Elementary	Capability	Capability to know and how to use E-commerce online payment platforms	Subtask	5
Number	Contents	Criteria			Score
1	Identification and understanding	To identify and understand popular international E-commerce online payment platforms			
2	Practices	To know how to use popular international online payment methods			

	3	Practices	To know the process of online shopping on websites and to know how to use international Alipay	
	4	Identification and understanding	To identify and understand popular services supported by WeChat and Alipay	
	5	Identification and understanding	To identify and understand security problems and solutions of E-commerce online payment	
		Total Score (1 point for each section)		
Test and Comments		Tutor Comments:		

Task Fulfillment Report

Title	
Class	Name	Student ID

Task Fulfillment Report

1. Present your task and your plan for it.
2. Present the difficulties you came across on completing the task and your solutions.
3. Present what you have learnt through all this process.

Write a report with no less than 200 words.

Scoring Criteria (10-score range)		
Tutor comments：	Attitude	
	Task Amount	

Scoring Rules

1. Timely finish all tasks.
2. Finish the tasks in reasonable way.
3. Reliable, coherent, logical and intelligible report.
4. Unfinished task will lead to 1 point deduction, and copy to 5 points deduction.

Keys

Exercise 1

1. VISA—维萨信用卡　　2. Escrow—第三方托管　　3. WeChat Pay—微信支付
4. UnionPay—银联支付　　5. MasterCard—万事达信用卡
6. Western Union—西联国际汇款
7. PayPal—贝宝

Exercise 2

1. 账户—account　　　　6. 电子支付—electronic payment
2. 余额—balance　　　　7. 移动支付—mobile phone payment
3. 订单—order　　　　　8. 第三方支付平台—third party online payment platform
4. 结算—settlement　　　9. 下单—make orders

5. 提现—withdrawal   10. 确认收货—confirm the delivery

Exercise 3

1. platforms   2. VISA；MasterCard   3. USD；RMB   4. line   5. multicurrency

Exercise 4

4
1
5
2
3
6

Unit 10

Cross-border E-commerce Logistics

Introduction

As we all know, CBEC emerging markets not only bring changes in retail industry, but also alter supply chain of logistics services. In this unit, we will learn about general knowledge of logistics including special FBA service in Amazon.com. Then we will discuss functions of overseas warehouses as well as learning about elements establishing an overseas warehouse. Lastly in supplementary reading, we will discover the advantages of overseas warehouses.

Contents

    Part A   An Introduction to Logistics Services
    Part B   Functions and How to Establish Overseas Warehouses
    Supplementary Reading

Learning Aims

- Learn about two main types of logistics services.
- Learn about advantages of FBA services in Amazon.
- Learn about functions of overseas warehouses and main factors to affect establish overseas warehouses.
- Learn about the advantages of overseas warehouses.

Capability Aims

- Be able to understand differentiation of types of logistics services.
- Be able to identify and understand FBA services in Amazon.
- Be able to identify overseas warehouses and understand functions of overseas warehouses.
- Be able to understand factors to affect establishing warehouses and advantages of having overseas warehouses.

Related Materials

Text A An introduction to Logistics Services

After you make orders on shopping platform, there are few things more satisfying than opening your front door to find a package with the items you purchased online two days or three days ago. But creating this kind of customers' satisfying experience requires a great deal of work behind the scenes by retailers. That is why E-commerce logistics companies should be required by merchants and customers. Nowadays E-commerce logistics are usually divided into two types, which are 1PL provider and 3PL provider.

We will talk about 1PL provider later. Firstly, 3PL sometimes is also called TPL and the full name is **third-party logistics**. It is interested to know and understand how E-commerce companies have been managing their distribution networks which consist of huge numbers of suppliers and customers. Globally most of companies prefer to choose E-commerce third-party logistics, which is an outsource logistic to a service provider. In industry terminology, as we all know, these service providers are also referred to as **3PLs**.

A full-service 3PL should satisfy all your logistics requirements, such as supply chain management, warehousing, consolidation service and order fulfillment. Therefore, participants get to perform roles that they specialize in an outsourcing to a third-party logistics provider who fits well with the E-commerce ecosystem. In China, Shunfeng, Yunda, Yuantong and Zhongtong are all third provider logistics companies and they are welcomed by all consumers around China.

However, nowadays in some online shopping platforms, E-commerce companies have set up their own distribution center and have been providing logistics services on their own. This service is called **first-party logistics** and is abbreviated as 1PL. 1PL service is attracting more and more customers and merchants now in China. For example, **Jindong (JD)** is one of the most popular online shopping platforms in China and JD started its 1PL service in 2007. In some backward areas, it even pioneers the **last-mile delivery service**. These models are still evolving and it is common to see that some parts of the logistics chain are outsourced to the logistics service providers and some parts being managed in-house.

As we mentioned above, the first-party logistics sometimes is also called **FBA service**. The services provided in FBA are similar to the service in self-built logistics. And speaking to setting up the own distribution center, **Amazon Business** is always a paradigm. FBA service in Amazon is referred as *Fulfillment By Amazon*. This is

Amazon's delivery service, which means the seller sends the goods to FBA's warehouse, and Amazon provides a range of services, including warehousing, picking up and packing, delivery, payment, customer service, and return. The core of FBA service is to let the sellers join in Amazon's logistics supply chain and they can store their goods in Amazon's logistics center, so as to enjoy Amazon's logistics services all over the world. That is why Amazon platform attaches great importance to the quality of sellers' logistics and after-sales service. More and more merchants choose to be a member in FBA service because FBA service is already achieving logistics standards in most <u>regions</u> and countries. As we know, it takes long time to send goods from China to Europe, and costs much. For Cross-border sellers, if they couldn't guarantee the reach of package to buyers in T-10 days, their reputation would be badly hurt. Therefore, choosing FBA service is a smart choice.

We cannot ignore the benefits of the process of logistics in Amazon. Amazon manages the entire logistics system so that it can serve itself. It <u>standardizes</u>, <u>modularizes</u> and serves its own logistics system so that the whole system can serve <u>external customers</u>. For example, in America, even if you are a small business owner, you can buy Amazon's FBA logistics service at a decent price, so as to complete what you want to do. This cooperation is named as **B2B** service. Amazon membership only requires $99 a year for **Prime** services so that you can enjoy all the membership services. One of the advantages of FBA logistics is that Amazon offers Prime members 2-day delivery and free shipping if they meet certain conditions. When Prime members order FBA products, they will be available on Amazon's shipping service on the next day or the second day, plus free shipping. Now more and more third-party sellers join in FBA services on Amazon. The more products FBA contains, the more valuable the Prime's price are.

Moreover, there are a number of advantages of FBA logistics. It has long-time warehousing and logistics experience and advanced <u>intelligent management system</u>. All of these can let buyers experience better logistics services. The <u>24 * 7 customer service</u> provided by FBA can solve the problem of real-time customer service communication for sellers. AS FBA establishes its own logistics at the same time, the seller does not need to worry about the bad reviews caused by logistics. In some regions of Europe, FBA services also increase export and delivery opportunities for orders from other countries.

Last but not least, there are disadvantages if you build up your own logistics service. While FBA improves the customer experience, it also requires sellers to pay higher delivery and warehousing costs, especially in warehousing. If the product is unmarketable, the seller will have to pay higher long-term storage fees. At the same time, FBA service is not responsible for <u>customs clearance</u> and transportation of goods from other countries to FBA warehouse, and the seller needs to solve the problem of head transportation. The FBA service makes it easy for buyers to return goods, which tends to cause higher return rates.

In addition, we talk about the costs of self-built logistics and also take FBA as an example. The cost of Amazon FBA logistics mainly includes storage fee and distribution fee. Storage fee is charged monthly and distribution fee is due to the size and weight of each product. The storage fee paid by the seller is divided into monthly storage fee and long-term storage fee. Monthly inventory warehousing fee is a monthly fee charged based on the size of the seller's goods when they arrive at the warehouse in the Amazon Logistics center. In addition to the monthly storage fee, the long-term storage fee is charged for the unsaleable evaluation of the storage time over 365 days. In order to avoid long-term storage charges, sellers should regularly monitor inventory status reports, submit removal orders for inventory that is about to expire, or conduct sales promotions to clear inventory in time. Items removed from inventory are returned to the seller by Amazon or disposed of by Amazon itself.

Questions

1. What is the definition of 3PLs?
2. What is the definition of self-distribution center service?
3. What are advantages and disadvantages of FBA service?

New Words and Terms

1. suppliers	n. 供应商	
2. customers	n. 消费者	
3. backward	adj. 落后的,滞后的	
4. pioneer	v. 开拓	
5. paradigm	n. 模范,范本	
6. regions	n. 地区	
7. standardize	v. 标准化	
8. modularize	v. 模块化	
9. inventory	n. 库存	
10. monitor	v. 监管	
11. clear	v. 移除	
12. dispose	v. 处理	
13. distribution networks	分销网络	
14. outsource logistics	外包物流	

续表

15. supply chain management	供应链管理
16. warehouse	仓储
17. consolidation service	综合服务
18. order fulfillment	订单管理
19. distribution center	配送中心
20. logistics chain	物流供应链
21. external customers	外部的客户群体
22. intelligent management system	智慧管理系统
23. customs clearance	海关清关
24. head transportation	头程运输
25. higher return rates	高退货率
26. storage fee	仓储费用
27. distribution fee	配送费用

Notes

1. third-party logistics：第三方物流，也称外包物流；很多跨境电商贸易公司使用的都是第三方物流；在中国，圆通、中通等快递公司都是优秀的第三方物流公司。

2. first-party logistics：第一方物流，也称自建物流；电商平台自建物流供应链也很常见，亚马逊就是自建物流，国内的京东是自建物流；自建物流有利也有弊。

3. Jindong：京东是国人熟知的与淘宝、天猫齐名的网购平台，同时还是国内少有的电商平台贸易综合体；京东平台是一个以零售为核心业务的平台型公司，京东快递也是国内比较优秀的自建物流公司。

4. last-mile delivery service：最后一公里物流服务；在偏远地区，第三方物流无法送达，京东快递做到了哪怕只差最后一公里也能送货上门的服务。

5. FBA service：亚马逊的代发货服务；亚马逊自营的 FBA 物流服务就是大家熟知的 Fulfillment By Amazon，这是亚马逊提供的代发货服务，是全球自建物流的一个典范，即卖家把货物发往 FBA 的仓库，亚马逊提供仓储、拣货打包、派送、收款、客服、退货处理等一系列服务，也就是说，FBA 提供的服务是让依附于亚马逊物流供应链上的商家可以将自己的货物寄存在亚马逊的物流中心，从而享受亚马逊遍布全球的物流服务；亚马逊平台非常看重卖家的物流配送和售后服务的质量，为了达到平台的物流标准，大部分卖家都建议使用 FBA 服务，尤其是欧洲市场的卖家，从国内寄往欧洲的商品物流时间长、费用高，如果卖家不能保证买家在 7~10 天里收到包裹，就会严重影响卖家的综合评分，这种情况下选择 FBA 发货是比较明智的做法。

6. Amazon Business：亚马逊也是全球综合贸易体的典范；Prime 会员服务、Marketplace

业务以及 AWS 亚马逊云服务是亚马逊的三大核心支柱,本章的主要内容是物流,所以这里主要讲解亚马逊的自建 FBA 代发货服务和 Prime 会员业务。

7. B2B:全称 Business to Business,即公司对公司的业务,在亚马逊 FBA 物流中较为常见;在美国,即使你是一个没有进驻亚马逊平台的小公司,也能以比较便宜的价格购买亚马逊的 FBA 物流服务,从而完成自己想做的事情,这就是现在物流行业的 B2B 业务。

8. Prime:亚马逊会员名称;亚马逊的用户每年只须支付 99 美元就可以享受 Prime 会员的各种服务,比如免邮费;FBA 物流的优点之一是亚马逊为 Prime 会员提供 2 日内送达服务和满足条件即可免运费的服务;Prime 会员下单购买使用 FBA 服务的商品,这些商品都会次日达或 2 日达,并且免运费,越多的第三方卖家使用 FBA 代发货服务,亚马逊快递覆盖的商品就越多,其 Prime 会员就越超值。

Abbreviations

3PL (Third-Party Logistics):第三方物流。
TPL (Third-Party Logistics):第三方物流。
1PL (First-Party Logistics):第一方物流。

Text B Functions of Overseas Warehouses and the Way to Establish them

In warehouse functions of logistics, overseas warehouses play an important role in supply chain of CBEC. Most of us might know the identification of warehouses but not everyone knows about overseas warehouses. In some cases, services in overseas warehouses bring more benefits and convenience than we expected. Some time there are reverse logistics happening. Actually, reverse logistics is also called *Return*. Take logistics service in Lazada as an example. Lazada has overseas warehouse operations in Shenzhen, Shenzhen within China. In the warehouse in Shenzhen, when a Chinese seller receives an order, it takes 5-11 days from the time the package arrives at the sorting center to the time the goods are delivered. Lazada is responsible for the logistics of the packages. If the delivery is failed, the package will be returned to Lazada's warehouse, which will then be returned to the overseas warehouse in Shenzhen. After the package arrives at the warehouse in Shenzhen, the seller will receive a return notice and the package will be returned to the seller from the overseas warehouse in Shenzhen. Therefore, we can conclude that having an overseas warehouse reduce the loss if reverse logistics occurs. In this article, we will talk about functions of warehouses and the factors related to setting up an overseas warehouse.

1. The reasons of setting up overseas warehouses

Therefore, why do you choose to set up overseas warehouse to serve your E-commerce customers? Here are two main reasons.

(1) After-sale Service

In an international transaction, E-commerce suppliers often feel helpless for after-sales service. According to the rules of the foreign service, customers do have the right to unconditionally return the products within a certain period of time. However, when a customer demands a return, returning delivery cost to where it started is really high. So, **the establishment of overseas warehouses will reduce the delivery costs and remove the concerns of customers**. At last, the customer can enjoy a high-quality after-sales service.

(2) Commodity Inspection and Customs Clearance

Commodity for export sometimes needs a long and complex procedure and when the goods arrive in target countries, the recipient has to pay for the tariff produced by customs clearance. Such a situation is not quite suitable for online shopping habits and is not favored by terminal customers. Hence, overseas warehouses could directly send the goods to customers, completely simplifying these procedures.

2. How to Build a Warehouse

When business companies are searching for the right place to secure their warehouse, they usually pay attention to two main features—**the space** that the warehouse can offer and **the location** of the warehouse. And also, there are other factors coming into play.

(1) Location

Figure out what you actually need the warehouse for, and storing goods is an obvious answer. Location is a prime factor when determining what warehouse to choose for and the location also determinate distributing and receiving goods. Therefore, it is important that your warehouse is situated in a location where it is convenient to ship goods to your customers. Good location means to have good transport routes such as railways or highways nearby. If you are a smaller, local business, then it will be wise to have a warehouse situated close to where your business is based. If you are a large business, your international warehouse should be centered on where most of your international customers are based. Moreover, when you have decided what location you require your warehouse to be established in, it is always good practice to evaluate the job market in the area to secure all the staff members you need.

Furthermore, the rent of the warehouse will inevitably influence your decision. And there are some aspects relating to costs which should play a part in your choice. Warehousing costs must cover the rent, equipment costs, fees of inventory management and so on. Warehousing fee also includes shipping fees, receiving fees, pick and pack fees. In a word, to incorporate all these factors, searching for a perfect warehouse is really connected to your financial planning.

(2) The Space

By linking warehouse operating to customer relationship management, business companies do manipulate sales and service personnel with real-time information to expand the business. Integration between a warehouse and an internal enterprise resource planning system needs more accurate planning and forecasting.

Furthermore, extending the warehouse to external partner systems can stimulate performance across the full supply chain ecosystem by collecting warehouse process and all stakeholders demand to achieve better cost-efficient improvement. Also, extending the warehouse increases the resilience of the supply chain network to adapt the changing conditions of marketing, such as changing from delays at an overseas factory to a satisfactory in customer demand.

As you can see, the perfect warehouse will be influenced by a wide range of factors. It is important that you take into consideration of them.

Questions

1. What are two main reasons to establish a warehouse?
2. What are two features you should consider to establish an overseas warehouse?

New Words and Terms

1. Return	n. 退货服务
2. commodity	n. 商品,货品
3. simplify	v. 简化
4. location	n. 选址
5. ecosystem	n. (物流)生态系统
6. resilience	n. (市场)弹性
7. overseas warehouse	海外仓
8. overseas warehouse operations	海外仓业务
9. sorting center	(货物)集散中心
10. international transaction	国际贸易,国际事务
11. customs clearance	海关清关
12. storing goods	仓储货物
13. warehousing costs	仓储成本

续表

14. shipping fees	物流运输费用
15. receiving fees	取货费用
16. pick and pack fees	打包费用
17. take into consider	考虑，考量

Notes

1. reverse logistics：逆向物流服务；除了常规的顺向物流服务以外，很多时候供应链会出现逆向物流服务，也叫退换货服务；以 Lazada 平台的物流仓储为例，Lazada 平台在中国香港、深圳和义务都设有海外仓业务，以中国香港的海外仓为例，中国卖家产生订单时，从包裹到达分拣中心再到货物妥投需要 5~11 天，这段路程的物流由 Lazada 负责；如果派送不成功，包裹会被退回 Lazada 当地的仓库，然后由当地的仓库退回到中国香港的海外仓，包裹抵达中国香港仓以后，卖家会收到退货通知，包裹会从中国香港仓退回卖家。

2. Lazada：来赞达，东南亚的著名电商平台，2017 年被中国的阿里巴巴公司收购。

3. the establishment of overseas warehouses will reduce the delivery costs and remove the concerns of customers：建立海外仓的主要优势在于跨境物流中本国海外仓的发货比同类型的境外发货更节省物流运费和成本，同时，缩短快递的运输时间也能减少买家的担忧和顾虑。

4. the space：空间开阔度；这是海外仓选址的一个重要因素；通过将仓库操作与客户关系管理联系起来，企业利用实时信息操纵销售和服务人员，以扩大业务；仓库与企业内部资源规划系统的集成需要更准确的规划和预测，这有助于形成一条更绿色的物流生态链。

5. the location：选址，这是建立海外仓的重要考虑因素，一般海外仓的选址都是以方便物流运输为准，如果仓库选址附近有高速、铁路等货运集散中心，这就是很好的要素。

Supplementary Reading

The Advantages of Overseas Warehouses

In a market research, more than half of the sellers want to build their own overseas warehouses. If the sellers sell more than one million dollars a month, the proportion of warehouses need even reach 69%. What are the advantages of setting up overseas warehouses in the Cross-border E-commerce export industry?

1. To Improve the Shopping Experience

Since products from overseas warehouses are directly delivered, it greatly shortens the delivery time. In local logistics, it is generally possible to check the status of goods online, through the whole process of tracking. And from the logistics tracking information, it is shipped from local area, not other places. Local delivery and distribution reduces the transshipment process and this method reduces the damage and packet loss rate. These factors will bring a good shopping experience to buyers.

2. To Reduce Logistics Costs

Postal packages and international logistics have certain restrictions on the weight, size and value of transported items, so large and valuable items can only be shipped by international courier. If any emergence happens, the overseas warehouse not only breaks through the restrictions on the weight, size and value of the goods, but also reduces the overall logistics price. It is equivalent to the price of the small package and it is at least 20% cheaper than international express.

3. To Gain Traffic Support from Platforms

The third-party trading platform will give more exposures and traffic support to the goods that are stored in their overseas warehouses.

4. To Expand Product Categories

Some products have long service period and are not fast-moving consumer products. But the market is needed and there are more profits if these products can be stored in overseas warehouses. There are no special restrictions on products in overseas warehouses. For some large-sized furniture, such as folding beds, the market competition of them will not be intense. So in this special products area it is still **a blue ocean** overseas.

5. To be Potential of Opening Up the Market

Overseas warehouses can be easily recognized by foreign buyers. If sellers pay attention to emerging markets, their products can not only be recognized by buyers, but also help sellers to accumulate more resources to open up new market and improve the product sales.

Overall, although overseas warehouses have many advantages in Cross-border logistics, they also have a great deal of requirement on sellers. For example, the seller needs to pay the storage fee and the storage fee costs in different countries and regions are different. Sometimes localized operations and management issues are complicated. It is expected that the benefits of having overseas warehouses overweigh all other unstable factors.

Notes

blue ocean：蓝海；商务英语和电商中的一个术语，泛指竞争不激烈的领域或品类，与红海意思相反，红海泛指竞争激烈的领域或品类。

Exercises

Task 1: Please compare two logistics models that are mentioned in text A and list their strengths and weaknesses in the following table.

Logistics Models	Strengths	Weakness
3PL model		
Self-distribution center		

Task 2: Please search online about the information of the following types of international logistics and fill in the table.

Logo of Internet Logistics	Chinese Name	Start from	Duration	Strengths and Weakness
DHL EXPRESS				
EMS				
FedEx				
中国邮政 CHINA POST				
TNT				
UPS				

Task 3: Suppose you were working for a domestic E-commerce platform and responsible for the export of electronics. Work in groups and select one or more cities in south-east Asia where you would like to establish warehouse. Please list out your reasons.

Exercises 1: Please match the following domestic online shopping platforms with its correct logistics service provider and "tick" in the right place.

	唯品会	天猫商城	京东平台	盒马
3PL Provider				
1PL Provider				

Exercises 2: Please translate the following words and phrases into English.

1. 供应商
2. 标准化
3. 监管
4. 外包物流
5. 配送中心
6. 退货
7. 市场弹性
8. 海关清关
9. 仓储货物
10. 打包

Exercises 3: Multiple choices.

1. Which of the following E-commerce platforms provides fulfillment service called "FBA"?

    A. eBay   B. Amazon   C. Alibaba

2. Which of the following statements is true about FBA?

    A. It provides storage and shipping service.
    B. It offers only storage space for your products.
    C. It doesn't cost anything if you register as a member.

3. Which of the following one might NOT be one of the services that FBA provides?

    A. Inventory management
    B. Customer service
    C. Sales analysis

Exercises 4: Please read the following sentences and choose whether the statements are true (T) or false (F).

_____ 1. FBA is the abbreviation of "Fulfillment by Administration".

_____ 2. With FBA service, sellers still need to manage their inventory.

_____ 3. If your customer asks for returning and refunds, FBA can deal with the problem.

_____ 4. FBA service fees depend largely on the size and weight of the products.

Exercises 5: Extension task— Is there any alternatives to FBA service? Please do the research online and discuss the results you got with your partner.

Learning Aims Achievement and Test

Section	Study on knowledge of logistics services including FBA services and everything about overseas warehouses	Class Hours		Course Credit	
Level	Medium	Capability	Capability to identify types of logistics, types of belonging in major platforms, benefits and functions of establishing overseas warehouses	Subtask	5

Number	Contents	Criteria	Score
1	Identification and understanding	To identify and understand different types of logistics services	
2	Practices	To identify of how procedures of FBA services run	
3	Practices	To know the features and benefits of FBA services	
4	Identification and understanding	To understand functions of overseas warehouses	
5	Identification and understanding	To understand factors of how to establish warehouses and advantages of establishing overseas warehouses	
	Total Score (1 point for each section)		
Test and Comments	Tutor Comments:		

Task Fulfillment Report

Title					
Class		Name		Student ID	
Task Fulfillment Report					

1. Present your task and your plan for it.
2. Present difficulties you came across on completing the task and your solutions.
3. Present what you have learnt through all this process.

Write a report with no less than 200 words.

Scoring Criteria (10-score range)		
Tutor comments：	Attitude	
	Task Amount	
Scoring Rules		

1. Timely finish all tasks.
2. Finish the tasks in reasonable way.
3. Reliable，coherent，logical and intelligible report.
4. Unfinished task will lead to 1 point deduction，and copy to 5 points deduction.

Keys

Exercise 1

唯品会—3PL Provider　　　天猫商城—3PL Provider

京东—1PL Provider　　　盒马—1PL Provider

Exercise 2

1. 供应商—suppliers
2. 标准化—standardize
3. 监管—monitor
4. 外包物流—outsource logistics
5. 配送中心—distribution center
6. 退货—Return
7. 市场弹性—resilience
8. 海关清关—customs clearance
9. 仓储货物—storing goods
10. 打包—pick and pack

Exercise 3

1. B
2. A
3. C

Exercise 4

1. F
2. T
3. T
4. F

Unit 11

Cross-border Customs Tax (VAT) and Changes in New E-commerce Regulations

Introduction

In all segments of Cross-border E-commerce, customs declaration is one of the most important procedures. Customs declaration usually contains declaration, inspection of goods, paying tax, releasing the goods and so on. During these procedures, Value Added Tax (VAT) is always widely mentioned. VAT usually means tax on profits from selling the products. Except a basic duty-free limit of sales, the rest of the sales amount must go to tax payment due to tax rate or tariff rate. According to the current laws, tax rate of VAT in different countries does have different values but most of countries' VAT rate is fluctuating at 20% of the goods value. Since 2009, new Cross-border E-commerce regulations have been implemented in China, so changes happened in customs declaration and VAT. In this unit, it will introduce functions of customs and VAT, major changes from new CBEC regulations and Frequently Answered Questions (FAQ) about VAT.

Contents

    Part A   An Introduction to Customs and VAT
    Part B   Changes of New E-commerce Regulations
    Supplementary Reading

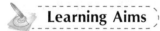

Learning Aims

- Learn about general knowledge of Customs and VAT.
- Learn about changes of new E-commerce regulations.
- Learn about proper solutions from Frequently Asked Questions in VAT.

Capability Aims

- Be able to know and understand definitions and functions of Customs and VAT.
- Be able to understand new benefits of the CBEC regulations after 2009.

- Be able to recognize the functions of Free Trade Zone (FTZ).
- Be able to recognize and practice the knowledge of VAT and CBEC regulations in practical work in the future.

Text A An introduction to Customs and VAT

As we all know, **the duty of Chinese customs** is to calculate both imported and exported goods, to inspect and analyze the goods scientifically and to implement efficient manipulation. Therefore, customs do play an important role in CBEC trade. In international trade, goods are transported into customs and they go through declaration, inspection and tax-paying. After all these procedures, customs ensure the goods are safe and it will release the goods. Once the goods are put into customs, they cannot be in trade. All the goods in international trade must go through customs to ensure they are legal. If customs find out the existence of forbidden objects, these objects will be distrained. If the value of amount of goods is out of free limit, the goods will be returned. There are circumstances out of your imagination happening in customs some time, the only thing you can do is to cooperate with staff members in customs in order to make everything going well.

It always occurs that the goods are distrained by customs for some reasons and the reasons are variable. If the goods value overweighs the application one and the goods need to be added more tax paying, if the goods belong to forbidden objects or even some goods copy ones that violates some protection laws and even sometimes the buyers cannot show any legal document to take away the goods, the goods need to stay in customs for a time. Please do not worry. We can negotiate with some solutions. If the goods need to be added more tax and the buyer refuses to pay it, the seller can give some discounts or coupons to the buyers to relieve their burden. Communication and cooperation are the best ways in E-commerce trade.

Now it is time to introduce VAT. VAT is the full name of **Value Added Tax**. It is originally from **European Union (EU)** and actually it is a kind of tax profit from goods sales. Paying VAT happens in business trade services either in import or in export within any region or country in EU. Moreover, VAT is divided into **Sales VAT and Import VAT**, separately. If the products are imported into overseas warehouses in EU, this situation comes to Import VAT. If the products have been sold in EU, this situation comes to sales VAT. There are exceptions. If the seller uses the goods in a local warehouse to sell the goods, it also belongs to sales VAT.

And even if the seller picks up overseas warehouse services that is third provided logistics, the seller still needs pay VAT. Furthermore, VAT has another two segments, which is **VAT number** and **VAT rate.** In order to pay VAT legally, the seller should apply for the VAT number in the local tax office where the warehouse belongs to and please remember that a VAT number is unique. According to the laws in EU, the VAT number is connected to the location of goods that belong to. If the seller applies for the VAT number in Britain, he can use overseas warehouses in Britain and he can mail the goods from Britain to other countries in EU. Nowadays on Amazon, eBay and Express, having a VAT number in Britain or in Germany is the entry for E-commerce trade.

In addition, speaking to tax rate in VAT, tax rate differs in categories of different products but most products' rate stays at 20% approximately. Also, the business trader needs pay VAT every three months due to the true **sales amount. In Britain VAT must be applied and being paid in a quarter of a year.** If there exists some surplus, **refund of VAT** occurs sometimes.

Overall, because cross border E-commerce is just emerging in these years, all the laws and regulations about VAT have been improved and have been becoming perfect. In Britain and Germany, governments require E-commerce platforms to share data and assist in tax enforcement to strengthen the management and verification of E-commerce tax payment.

Questions

1. What is the definition of VAT?
2. What are two tax segments of VAT?
3. What are two forms of tax refund of VAT?

New Words and Terms

1. procedure	n. 程序,手续
2. fluctuate	v. (在一定值范围内)浮动
3. distrain	v. 扣留,扣押
4. variable	adj. 多样化的
5. violate	v. 违法,侵犯
6. import	v. 进口
7. export	v. 出口
8. exception	n. 例外
9. segment	n. 部分,环节
10. unique	adj. 唯一的,独一无二的
11. enforcement	n. 实施,执行

续表

12. verification	n. 证明，证实
13. customs declaration	海关报关，海关清关
14. forbidden object	违禁物品
15. communication and cooperation	沟通与合作
16. sales amount	销售额
17. tax payment	缴税，税收

Notes

1. the duty of Chinese customs：中国海关的职责；海关的职责在跨境贸易中非常重要，海关主要对货物进行贸易统计，负责对进出中国关境的货物进行统计调查和分析，以科学、准确地反映对外贸易的运行态势，实施有效的统计监督；国际贸易中的任何货物在进入海关时都需要进行申报、查验和缴税，确认无误后海关才会放行；货物在清关期间受海关监管，不可以自由流通；所有跨境包裹都需要经过海关，海关对每个包裹都会进行检查，违禁物品会被海关扣留，货值超过免税标准的会被征税，未正常缴税的会被退回。

2. Value Added Tax（VAT）：售后增值税，这原本是欧盟的一种税制，是货物售价的利润税，适用于在欧盟国家境内产生的进口、商业交易及服务行为。

3. Sales VAT and Import VAT：在商品进口到欧盟国家的海外仓时会产生商品的进口增值税，而商品在其境内销售时会产生销售增值税；如果卖家使用欧盟国家本地仓进行发货，就属于销售增值税应缴范畴，即使卖家所选的海外仓储服务是由第三方物流公司提供的，也需要缴纳 VAT 税。

4. VAT number：VAT 税号，每个 VAT 税号都是唯一的；一旦申请到税号，卖家就需要按照实际销售金额和法律规定的时间进行税务申报。

5. VAT rate：根据各国的现行税率，不同类目的产品的 VAT 增值税税率各不相同，但绝大多数产品的税率在 20% 左右。

6. In Britain VAT must be applied and being paid in a quarter of a year：以英国为例，VAT 需要卖家按季度申报，每个 VAT 税号每三个月需要向英国税务海关总署（HMRC）进行一次当季进口和销售情况的申报，以结算本季度 VAT 税号名下产生的所有进口增值税和销售增值税。

7. refund of VAT：VAT 退税；季度申报 VAT＝销售增值税－进口增值税，销售增值税大于进口增值税则需要缴纳额外的销售增值税，反之则退返超出的进口增值税；退税的形式有两种，以支票形式退还或直接退回到 VAT 账户，当作余额留在下一季度需要缴纳销售增值税时抵扣。

Abbreviations

VAT：Value Added Tax，增值税的简称。

CBEC: Cross-border Electronic Commerce,跨境电商的简称。
EU: European Union,欧盟的简称。

Text B Changes in New E-commerce Regulations

There have been new changes since 2009 because several Chinese government institutions, including **the Ministry of Commence**, **the Ministry of Finance** and the **General Administration of Customs** all agreed to implement the aforementioned regulation on that year. The new regulation as well as the new CBEC regulations has taken effect from January 1, 2009.

Firstly, changes bring more benefits available. The new CBEC regulations do create new benefits to strengthen the incentives to purchase through the CBEC channel. All the new benefits are as follows.

One of the most significant benefits is that it expands more choices of pre-importation registration waiver. The new CBEC regulations indefinitely extend the waiver of the pre-importation registration requirements on specified categories of products such as cosmetics, infant formula milk, healthy food, medical devices and so on, which was originally set to expire on December 31, 2018. As pre-importation registration belongs to an important part of the current regime to impose Chinese national standards on certain sensitive foreign products, this waiver continues to allow products, which may not be available through the ordinary commercial channel due to market entry barriers, to be imported through the CBEC channel.

Another benefit is more tariff exemption and tax reduction. The current tax policy under which customs duties are exempted and import VAT and consumption taxes are collected at a 30% discount for the products imported through the CBEC channel continues to be implemented.

Furthermore, the new regulations do expand positive lists. The scope of the positive lists is expanded to include 63 new tariff categories, which contains the tariff categories for the products permitted to be sold through the CBEC channel.

In addition, we can have more **Free Trade Zone** (**FTZ**) distribution center in China. The new CBEC regulations continue to allow a foreign seller to stockpile products in one of the FTZs in China, from which the seller can satisfy customer orders and deliver the products directly to the end consumers. This method gives overseas sellers a more efficient delivery option, compared with the alternative option of international parcel delivery. On the contrary, sellers not enrolled in the CBEC program are not permitted to sell their products directly from an FTZ in China to Chinese consumers.

Last but not least, the new regulations do bring about new compliance responsibilities imposed by the CBEC. Firstly, while after-sales services and consumer protection have been becoming more variable under the new regulations, the CBEC program must designate a Chinese responsible party which will be held directly by the Chinese authorities for consumer complaints, product recalls and other product quality or safety obligations. Secondly, there are new challenges in customs compliance. With respect to customs compliance, the new CBEC regulations stress the prohibition against redistribution of the products imported through the CBEC channel. All entrepreneurs and local sellers should cooperate with customs in investigating violations involving redistribution and customs has also put into effect IT infrastructure to ensure that the buyers' information on the import declaration documents is reconciled with the payment information processed by the payment service providers. Thirdly, quality requirements are becoming more and more regulated and general product safety is becoming more and more important. Based on the observation, customs authorities and domestic market regulators are still actively conducting flexible inspection and testing of the CBEC products on a selective basis in terms of their compliance with the Chinese national standards. However, such enforcement do play significant role in human safety and health implications.

Questions

1. What are three changes of benefits that the new regulations bring into?
2. What are new three responsibilities imposed by the CBEC?

New Words and Terms

1. incentive	n. 动机,鼓励,激励
2. waiver	n. 豁免
3. expire	v. 失效
4. regime	n. 管理体制
5. exempt	v. 免除
6. stockpile	v. 储存,贮存
7. compliance	n. 遵循,服从
8. violation	n. 违反
9. reconcile	v. 和解,调停
10. enforcement	n. 实施,执行
11. tariff exemption	免除缴税
12. tax reduction	减少征税
13. consumption taxes	消费税

续表

14. positive lists	允许进口的货品清单
15. overseas sellers	海外卖家，境外的卖家
16. parcel delivery	包裹运输，快递运输
17. after-sales services	售后服务
18. consumer protection	消费者权益保护
19. product recalls	产品召回（适用于出现质量等问题的产品）
20. product quality	产品质量
21. safety obligations	安全责任
22. human safety	人体安全
23. health implications	健康隐患

Notes

1. the Ministry of Commerce：商务部，主要职责为拟订国内外贸易和国际经济合作的发展战略、政策，起草国内外贸易、外商投资、对外援助、对外投资和对外经济合作的法律法规草案及制定部门规章等。

2. the Ministry of Finance：财政部，主要职责为拟订财税发展战略、规划、政策和改革方案并组织实施，分析预测宏观经济形势，参与制定各项宏观经济政策等。

3. General Administration of Customs：海关总署，主要职责为负责全国海关工作，包括拟订海关（含出入境检验检疫，下同）工作政策，起草相关法律法规草案；负责组织推动口岸"大通关"建设，会同有关部门制定口岸管理规章制度，组织拟定口岸发展规划；负责海关监管工作；制定进出境运输工具、货物和物品的监管制度等。

4. Free Trade Zone (FTZ)：自由贸易区的统称和简称，通常指两个以上的国家和地区通过签订自由贸易协定，相互取消绝大部分货物的关税和非关税壁垒，取消大多数服务部门的市场准入限制，开放投资，从而促进商品、服务和资本、技术、人员等生产要素的自由流动，实现优势互补，促进共同发展；自由贸易区按性质可分为商业自由区和工业自由区；按功能类型可分为转口集散型、贸工结合型、以贸为主型、出口加工型和保税仓储型。

Abbreviations

CBEC：Cross-border Electronic Commerce，跨境电商的简称。
FTZ：Free Trade Zone，自由贸易区，保税区。
IT：Information Technology，信息技术的简称。

Supplementary Reading

Frequently Asked Questions（FAQ）and Suggested Answers in VAT

In the market research, VAT problems are inevitable. With some mistake usage, the seller's account number will be locked and the sellers will lose the rights of sales. Facing changes and new situation, if the sellers run the business trade legally and systematically, they will have new chances to get better development. Now there are some frequently asked questions about VAT with suggestions and answers as follows.

(1) What are the consequences if the seller does not apply for a VAT number and refuse to pay VAT?

According to the regulations of **Tax in Britain**, one single trade account number must apply for a VAT number and the seller must provide for valid information to make the VAT number validity. If anyone put in invalid information, he will get penalty from government.

(2) What about a business owner use another one's VAT number for application? Can two or three separate account numbers bond to the same VAT number?

Every VAT number is unique. As a seller, you should apply for your own unique VAT number and this true unique VAT number is your business running guarantee. Misusing or abusing a VAT number will lead to consequences and the seller will get serious penalty from tax department.

(3) If I am just a small business owner, can I escape the step of applying for the VAT number to run my business?

Of course not. According to the requirements of tax in Britain, if you are a seller in online sales, you should apply for a VAT number and pay VAT every three months, regardless of the scale of your business or the scale of the owner.

(4) What kind of resources and papers should the seller prepare for a quarter of a year's VAT application?

For a quarter's VAT application, you should prepare for these documents. Firstly, it is entry document, which means the document list of imported VAT payment. Secondly, it is bank statement bill provided by logistics companies. Thirdly, it is sales documents, which include the bill receipt to guests, sales statistics in PayPal or monthly bank statement. Fourthly, it is the list of goods purchasing and other necessary receipts. In a word, all the documents should be well-prepared.

(5) If I have a VAT number in Britain, can I use this VAT number to run services in other overseas warehouse in EU or in FBA service?

It is mentioned that a VAT number in Britain can be used in other countries of EU only if the goods are transformed in warehouses in Britain for sales firstly. According to the tax law in EU, the location of overseas warehouses where the goods belong to be bonded to local VAT number. If a Chinese company applies for a VAT number in Britain, this number cannot be used in other regions or countries in EU.

(6) Can I use direct mail within China to escape paying VAT?

According to tax law in EU, VAT free is only for a single product's value under 15 pounds or under 22 euros. If the value is over these two prices, VAT is needed to pay. Even if the declared value is not consistent with the object, resulting in the seizure of the parcel by the customs, goods will be required to pay VAT as soon as possible.

Notes

tax in Britain: 英国税法; 现在跨境电商中VAT的出现和使用频率最高的地方是英国, 所以本文中的所有建议和回答都会优先以英国的跨境电商贸易为例。

Exercises

Task 1: According to the new CBEC regulations in Text B, please discuss the following operations with your partner and choose the ones that are permitted now.

1. A Canadian seller can deliver his goods directly from an FTZ in China to Chinese consumers.

2. Chinese importers' goods don't need to be inspected.

3. The customs can get access to a CBEC seller's transaction data.

4. A British seller conducts a Chinese partner to deal with the after-sales services in China.

The permitted operations are _____.

Task 2: Please search online to find out the locations of the Cross-border E-commerce Free Trade Zone (FTZ) establish in 2018 to fill in the table and also find out their unique policies for E-commerce companies to fill in the table.

Locations of FTZ in 2018	Policies

Task 3: Please search online or visit a Hema store to find out the similarities and differences between Hema stores and traditional supermarkets and write them down below.

Similarities	Differences

Reading Comprehensions

Please read the passage below and answer the following answers.

Have you ever thought any legal issues that E-commerce platforms may face? It should be less serious than a physical store so we don't need to worry too much about them. Customers meet website owner anyway. In that case, it's totally wrong. Running an online business does not mean you can escape legal matters. Can you name these legal issues? First of all, it's data protection and privacy. E-commerce platforms are just like reservoirs of sensitive customer reservation. Most often collected by customer registration and even during payments for purchases. E-commerce platforms are obliged to protect these data and requirements for legal compliance. In the European Union, E-commerce website is required by the General Data Protection Regulation (GDPR) to notify their users when they gather users' information and seek explicit consent before collecting or reusing personal data.

To ensure the website is compliant with data protection rules, you should start by creating comprehensive data protection policies in addition to your cooky policy. These policies should be clearly visible on your website as well. What about you really do get hacked? Payment fraud has become quite popular over the years. One report projected that card-not-present frauds will grow by 40% annually up to 2023. If you get hacked, you are then legally obliged to inform the public. Many countries require businesses to report any bridge to the public. In addition to protect customers' information on your website, it is important to go to deeper into inner-working of your E-commerce site to prevent the fraud. One preventing way is Application Performance Management (APM). And apart from data protection which has been discussed, other issues such as trademark security issues, copyright protection or intellectual property are also some crucial issues you need pay attention to.

1. Multiple choices.

1) What does the passage mainly talk about?

    A. Some legal issues one might face when conducting an E-commerce business

    B. Why the domain name of the E-commerce website is easily hacked

C. How to obtain customers' personal data

2) Which of the following is NOT one of the legal issues mentioned in the passage?

A. Trademark security

B. Data protection and privacy

C. Contract problems

3) According to the passage, which of the following statements is NOT correct in terms of data protection and privacy?

A. E-commerce websites are required to notify the users only when user data is leaked

B. It is important to create clear and visible data protection policies on the website

C. If user information is really leaked, the website owner needs to inform the public

2. According to the passage, please decide whether the statements are true (T) or false (F).

_____ 1) Website owners would encounter fewer legal issues than physical store owners do.

_____ 2) Most E-commerce platforms collect customer information through online survey.

_____ 3) It is reported that the number of card-not-present frauds is growing.

_____ 4) APM can be used to ensure your website runs smoothly.

Learning Aims Achievement and Test

Section	Study on Customs and VAT	Class Hours		Course Credit	
Level	Academic	Capability	Capability to know and use the knowledge of VAT and the new CBEC regulations in practice	Subtask	4

Number	Contents	Criteria	Score
1	Identification and understanding	To identify and understand functions of Customs and VAT	
2	Understanding	To understand new benefits of the CBEC regulations created in 2009	
3	Identification and understanding	To identify and understand functions of Free Trade Zone (FTZ)	
4	Practice	To use the knowledge of VAT and new customs regulations to solve practical problems	

	Total Score (1 point for each section)
Test and Comments	Tutor Comments:

Task Fulfillment Report

Title	
Class	Name	Student ID
Task Fulfillment Report	

1. Present your task and your plan for it.
2. Present the difficulties you came across on completing the task and your solutions.
3. Present what you have learnt through all this process.

Write a report with no less than 200 words.

Tutor comments:	Scoring Criteria (10-score range)	
	Attitude	
	Task Amount	
Scoring Rules		

1. Timely finish all tasks.
2. Finish the tasks in reasonable way.
3. Reliable, coherent, logical and intelligible report.
4. Unfinished task will lead to 1 point deduction, and copy to 5 points deduction.

Keys

Exercise 1

1. C
2. C
3. A

Exercise 2

1. F
2. F
3. T
4. T

Unit 12
ERP and Supply Chain of Cross-border E-commerce

Introduction

This unit is divided into two parts. The first part focuses on ERP including its concept, advantages, features, different modules and Cross-border E-commerce ERP platforms. The second part is about supply chain, including its concept, functions, basic elements, flows, supply chain management and its advantages, as well as Cross-border E-commerce supply chain platforms.

Contents

Part A   ERP
Part B   Supply Chain

Learning Aims

- Acquire the basic knowledge about the concept, advantages, features and different modules of ERP.
- Acquire the basic knowledge about the concept, functions, basic elements and flows of supply chain.
- Acquire the basic knowledge about supply chain management and its advantages.
- Know some Cross-border E-commerce ERP platforms.
- Know some Cross-border E-commerce supply chain platforms.
- Learn words, phrases, expressions and terms in this unit about ERP and supply chain.

Capability Aims

- Be able to talk in English about the basic information covered in this unit concerning ERP and supply chain.
- Be able to identify the key factors in choosing an effective ERP platform.
- Be able to identify the key factors in choosing an effective supply chain platform.

 **Related Materials**

Part A ERP

1. The Concept and Advantages of ERP

ERP (Enterprise Resource Planning) is a management platform to provide employees and decision-makers with decision methods through integrating information technology with advanced and systematic management <u>ideology</u>. It is also an enterprise information management system that provides integrated <u>cross-region</u>, cross-department and even cross-company real-time information. ERP is not only a software but also a management ideology, which has realized the integration of enterprise's <u>interior</u> resources with enterprise-related <u>exterior</u> resources. It closely integrates the enterprise's people, <u>property</u>, products, production, supply and distribution with related logistics, information flow, <u>fund flow</u>, management flow and value-added flow to achieve resource optimization and sharing.

ERP is a new-generation integrated management system <u>evolving from</u> MRP. Its core ideology is supply chain management. <u>Surpassing</u> the limit of traditional enterprises, ERP has optimized the enterprise's resources from the <u>scope</u> of supply chain and the <u>running mode</u> of modern enterprises. It has also reflected the enterprise's requirements of <u>rational</u> resource allocation. It has a significant effect on improving the enterprises' business processes and their core competitiveness.

2. The Features of ERP

(1) Practicability

It aims at <u>overall</u> balancing and optimal management of an enterprise's comprehensive resources such as people, property, products, information, time, space and so forth. It <u>coordinates</u> the enterprise's each management department and organizes business activities based on market <u>orientation</u>. It is devoted to improve the enterprise's core competitiveness.

(2) Integration

The typical feature of ERP is to integrate all the enterprise's information systems. It is more functional than the traditional single system.

(3) Flexibility

It adopts <u>modular</u> design, which enables the system itself to support and integrate new modules according to the enterprise's needs, improving the enterprise's <u>adaptability</u>.

(4) Data storage

It integrates data originally scattering in each corner of the enterprise to ensure its consistency and improve its accuracy and precision.

(5) Convenience

Because of integration, information produced within the enterprise can be obtained and applied everywhere in the enterprise through this system.

(6) Appraisal management

ERP makes lateral ties efficient and close, which improves the appraisal management.

(7) Interaction

Through ERP, the enterprise and the suppliers of raw materials are closely connected, increasing its market adaptability. While **CRM** enables the enterprise to fully master the orientation of market needs. Both ERP and CRM are conducive to developing interactive relations between the enterprise and its suppliers & consumers.

(8) Real-time

ERP is the integrated management of all the enterprise information. The key of integration lies in "real-time and dynamic management". All the management problems in real work are about department coordination and post matching. Therefore, ERP without "real-time dynamic management methods and management capability" is empty talk.

(9) Immediacy

The key of ERP management is the "informationization of real work". Namely, the real work content and work mode are displayed through informationized means. Because of limited capability and energy, people may make mistakes when the real work becomes so complex. To informationize the work content and work mode will develop the informationized system of ERP management, which will equip the enterprise with reliable informationized management tool.

3. The Different Modules of ERP

(1) Accounting

Accounting module mainly achieves the functions like recording cashier software, adjusting accounts, reflecting and analyzing asset management, and so forth.

(2) Financial management

Financial management module mainly achieves the analysis, prediction, management and control of financial data through accounting function. Because of the financial management demands, the type selection of ERP should focus on the control, analysis and prediction of procurement, storage and sale in financial planning.

(3) Manufacturing control management

Manufacturing control management module is the core of cashier software system. It combines an enterprise's whole manufacturing processes, enabling the enterprise to effectively lower inventory and improve efficiency. The enterprise finishes the ERP type selection based on its own development needs, then connects procurement, storage and sale to make the manufacturing process consistent.

(4) Logistics management

Logistics management module focuses on the costs of logistics. It takes advantage of the benefit relations among logistics elements to organize logistics activities scientifically and rationally. Through effective ERP type selection, it can control and lower the costs of logistics, which will improve the economic benefits of the enterprise and society.

(5) Procurement management

Procurement management module can ensure order quantity, confirm supplier and product safety. It also provides functions including supplier information searching, purchasing, price planning and so forth. It promises timely delivery of goods by providing information like ordering, inspection & acceptance, and tracking.

(6) Distribution management

Distribution management module mainly manages and counts the information like products, regions and customers. It also analyzes sales volume, sales amount, profits, appraisal, customers and so forth.

(7) Inventory control

Inventory control module is used to control and manage stored goods. It is a dynamic and real inventory control system, which can adjust inventory according to department demands and precisely show the inventory situation.

(8) HR management

Previous ERP system focused on manufacturing and selling processes. With the development of human resources, HR management has become an independent module. It has been added to the ERP system to be combined with financial and manufacturing system to form an efficient and highly integrated enterprise resource system. It includes recruitment management, wage accounting, and so forth.

4. Cross-border E-commerce ERP Platforms

The fast-growing Cross-border E-commerce has given birth to a number of ERP platforms, such as ASINKING, ActNeed, Mabang ERP and so forth.

ASINKING, headquartered in Shenzhen, is a service provider focusing on Cross-border ERP. It is also a one-stop management system for Amazon sellers. It is devoted to providing Cross-border E-commerce sellers with accurate, complete and multi-dimensional real-time data. It assists sellers in improving efficiency and optimizing flows of sales, inventory, ads, customer service, and operation management. It not only displays sales data and serves as an operation tool, but also provides sellers with a perfect functional management of the whole supply chain. It markedly improves sellers' working efficiency, enabling them to maintain the increase of businesses while investing more time in developing their company.

ActNeed platform provides sellers with multi-language product translation, Amazon quick publishing, multi-store unified management, product management, order management and so forth. This platform enables user to effectively and quickly finish all the daily routines, greatly improving working efficiency. Currently, this ERP supports some popular Cross-border E-commerce platforms like Amazon, AliExpress, eBay, Wish, Lazada, DHgate and so forth.

Mabang ERP is the earliest domestic Cross-border ERP. Its main functions including product publishing, orders, products, warehouse, FBA, logistics, customer service, procurement management, staff appraisal and so forth. It is not only an ERP software, but also a comprehensive Cross-border E-commerce service platform. Besides, it provides many online paid apps and ERP modules. This ERP also supports some mainstream Cross-border E-commerce platforms like Amazon, eBay, Wish, AliExpress and so forth.

Questions
1. What is ERP?
2. What are the main modules of ERP?
3. What are the advantages of ERP?

Notes

CRM：Customer Relationship Management，即客户关系管理，是企业为提高核心竞争力，利用相应的信息技术以及互联网技术协调企业与顾客在销售、营销和服务上的交互，从而提升其管理方式，向客户提供创新式的个性化客户交互和服务的过程，其终极目标是吸引新客户、保留老客户以及将已有客户转化为忠实客户。

New Words and Terms

1. ideology	n. 理念
2. cross-region	adj. 跨区域的
3. interior	adj. 内部的
4. exterior	adj. 外部的
5. property	n. 物产；财产
6. surpass	v. 超越；超过

7. scope	n. 范围
8. rational	adj. 理性的；合理的
9. overall	adj. 总体的
10. coordinate	v. 协调
11. orientation	n. 方向
12. modular	adj. 模块的
13. adaptability	n. 应变能力；适应性
14. storage	n. 存储
15. scatter	v. 分散
16. lateral	adj. 横向的
17. appraisal	n. 考核
18. interaction	n. 交互性
19. reliable	adj. 可靠的
20. accounting	n. 会计核算
21. cashier	n. 收银员
22. asset	n. 资产
23. procurement	n. 采购
24. recruitment	n. 招聘
25. mainstream	adj. 主流的
26. fund flow	资金流
27. evolve from	由…衍化而来
28. running mode	经营模式
29. raw materials	原材料
30. be conducive to	对…有益
31. post matching	岗位匹配
32. benefit relations	效益关系

Exercises

Task 1: Complete the following sentences with the words or phrases in the box.

surpass	rational	orientation	storage	asset
procurement	recruitment	reliable	evolve from	be conducive to

1. _____ process is one of the ways to control staff's English ability from the beginning and build English competitiveness.
2. Miller was a quiet and _____ man.
3. They moved to a house with lots of _____ space.
4. Chairs in rows are not as _____ to discussion as chairs arranged in a circle.
5. It's impossible to have a _____ conversation with him.
6. Each party shall be prepared to explain to any other party its government _____ procedures.
7. He has _____ all our expectations.
8. Fish _____ prehistoric sea creatures.
9. Her _____ include shares in the company and a house in France.
10. The company needs to develop a stronger _____ towards marketing its products.

Task 2: Translate the following sentences into Chinese.
1. It closely integrates the enterprise's people, property, products, production, supply and distribution with related logistics, information flow, fund flow, management flow and value-added flow to achieve resource optimization and sharing.
2. Surpassing the limit of traditional enterprises, ERP has optimized the enterprise's resources from the scope of supply chain and the running mode of modern enterprises.
3. It coordinates the enterprise's each management department and organizes business activities based on market orientation.
4. It adopts modular design, which enables the system itself to support and integrate new modules according to the enterprise's needs, improving the enterprise's adaptability.
5. Distribution management module mainly manages and counts the information like products, regions and customers. It also analyzes sales volume, sales amount, profits, appraisal, customers and so forth.

Part B Supply Chain

1. About Supply Chain

Supply chain is a network chain structure that connects the supplier, manufacturer, distributor and the final customer. Supply chain starts from kits, then manufactures intermediate and final products. Finally the sales network sends these products to the consumers. The functions of a supply chain include product development, marketing, operations, distribution, finance, and customer services.

The basic elements of supply chain include the supplier, manufacturer, distribution enterprise, retail enterprise and consumer. The supplier refers to the enterprises that provide the manufacturers with raw materials or components and parts. The manufacturer is the product manufacturing, which is the most important process of production. It is mainly responsible for the production, development and after-sales services. The distribution enterprise is the product circulation agent enterprise aiming at sending the products to every corner of the scope of business. Retail enterprise is the enterprise that sells products to the consumers. Consumer is the final process of supply chain, and the only source of income for the whole supply chain.

Supply chain has four flows including material circulation, business circulation, information circulation and fund circulation. Each flow has its own functions and circulation directions. For material circulation, it is the circulation process of materials (goods), and a procedure of sending goods. The direction of this flow is from supplier to consumer through manufacturer, wholesale and logistics, retailer, and so forth. For business circulation, it is mainly about the circulation process of selling and buying. It is a business process about accepting orders, signing contracts, and so forth. The direction of this flow is a two-way flow between supplier and consumer. The forms of business circulation are diverse with traditional store sales, door-to-door sales, mail orders and E-commerce sales. For information circulation, it is a process about goods and transaction information. The direction of this flow is also a two-way flow between supplier and consumer. In the past, people mainly focused on material goods, while the information circulation is neglected. For the fund circulation, it is the circulation of currency. To guarantee the normal operation of an enterprise, timely fund recovery must be ensured. Otherwise, the enterprise cannot establish a perfect operation system. The direction of this flow is from consumer to supplier through retailer, wholesale and logistics, manufacturer, and so forth.

With the establishment of supply chain, it will gradually improve the satisfaction of customers and the management of the enterprise, save transaction costs, reduce inventory and procurement costs, facilitate the management of supplier, decrease cycling period, increase income & profit, and expand network.

2. Supply Chain Management and Its Advantages

Supply chain management (SCM) is an advanced management ideology. Its advanced nature lies in its customer and final consumer-oriented ideology as well as a manufacturing and supplying mode based on meeting the ultimate requirements of customers and consumers. Besides, supply chain management has the following features. First, it is market and customer demand-oriented. Based on win-win principle, its targets are improving competitiveness, market share, customer satisfaction, and maximum profit. Second, it operates on coordinated business and competition, achieving effective planning and control of the whole supply chain's information flow, logistics, fund flow, business flow and value flow through the application of modern enterprise management technology, information technology and integration technology. Finally, it forms an extremely competitive strategic alliance and a whole network structure connecting customer, supplier, manufacturer, seller, service provider and all the other cooperation partners. In essence, supply chain management delves into every appreciation process of supply chain, and then send the right product to the right place according to the right time, right quantity, right quality and right status (6R), achieving the minimum total cost. Supply chain management is a crucial process because an optimized supply chain results in lower costs and a faster production cycle.

Supply chain management includes planning, purchasing, manufacturing, distributing and goods returning. For planning, it is a strategic part of supply chain management. A strategy is needed to manage all the resources to meet the customers' needs for your products. A good plan is to establish a series of methods to monitor supply chain, enabling it to send high-quality and high-value products or services to customers effectively and with low cost. For purchasing, it chooses a supplier that can provide products and services with related goods. It establishes a set of processes including price fixing, distributing and paying, then creates methods to monitor and improve management. It then combines those processes with the management process of the goods and services provided by the supplier, including picking up the goods, checking shipping list, transferring goods to the manufacturing department as well as approving the payment to supplier. For manufacturing, it involves arranging production, testing, packing, and the activities about delivery preparation. This part has the most measurement in supply chain including quality level, product output, workers' production efficiency, and so forth. For distributing, it is about adjusting the users' order receipt, establishing warehouse network, sending deliverymen to pick up goods and send to the customers, setting commodity pricing system and receiving payment. For goods returning, it is the supply chain's problems-solving part. It establishes networks to receive the consumers' returned defective goods and surplus products, and provide support when the consumers encounter problems of using the products.

3. Cross-border E-commerce Supply Chain Platforms

The fast-growing Cross-border E-commerce has not only given birth to a number of ERP platforms, but also some supply chain platforms such as Alibaba Cross-border supply chain.

Alibaba Cross-border supply chain is a platform of Alibaba Group. It is the world's leading one-stop Cross-border supply chain service platform. It is based on big data, cloud computing, and **SaaS**. It integrates Alibaba's internal and external resources like global banks, financial institutions, logistics service providers, **customs brokers**,

Cai Niao network, **Ant financial service** and other resources. It aims at providing one-stop services for small and medium-sized enterprises on Alibaba.com such as foreign trade comprehensive services like <u>smart</u> customs clearance platform, <u>trade assurance</u>, international logistics, financial services like payment & settlement, and supply chain finance. It makes foreign trade become easier.

Questions

1. What is the supply chain?
2. What are the basic elements of supply chain?
3. What is supply chain management and its advantages?

Notes

1. SaaS：Software-as-a-Service，软件即服务，是一种软件布局模型，专为网络交付而设计；SaaS 提供商为企业搭建信息化所需的所有网络基础设施及软件、硬件运作平台，并负责所有前期的实施、后期的维护等一系列服务，企业无须购买软硬件、建设机房、招聘 IT 人员，即可通过互联网使用信息系统。
2. customs broker：报关行，是指经海关准予注册登记，接受进出口货物收发货人的委托，以进出口货物收发货人或者自己的名义向海关办理代理报关业务，从事报关服务的境内企业。
3. Cai Niao network：菜鸟网络，指由阿里、顺丰、三通一达（申通、圆通、中通、韵达）等共同组建的菜鸟网络科技有限公司，它不是一家物流公司，它可以让仓储、快递、运输、落地配送等环节的合作伙伴获得更清晰的业务场景，并使用数据获得更好的生产能力。
4. Ant Financial service：蚂蚁金融服务集团，简称蚂蚁金服，起步于 2004 年成立的支付宝；小微金融（筹）是蚂蚁金服的前身；蚂蚁金服以"让信用等于财富"为愿景，致力于打造开放的生态系统，以移动互联、大数据、云计算为基础，为中国践行普惠金融的重要实践，旗下有支付宝、余额宝、招财宝、蚂蚁聚宝、网商银行、蚂蚁花呗、芝麻信用等业务板块。

New Words and Terms

1. kit	n. 配套设备
2. intermediate	adj. 中间的；中级的
3. flow	n. 流程
4. procedure	n. 步骤
5. diverse	adj. 多种多样的
6. neglect	v. 忽略
7. currency	n. 货币

续表

8. consumer-oriented	adj. 以消费者为中心的
9. ultimate	adj. 最终的
10. maximum	adj. 最大化的
11. alliance	n. 联盟
12. appreciation	n. 增值
13. status	n. 状态；地位
14. minimum	adj. 最小化的
15. crucial	adj. 至关重要的
16. approve	v. 审批；批准
17. output	n. 产量
18. receipt	n. 收据
19. surplus	adj. 过剩的；剩余的
20. smart	adj. 智能的
21. components and parts	零部件
22. product circulation	产品流通
23. agent enterprise	代理企业
24. sign contract	签合同
25. fund recovery	资金回收
26. in essence	实质上
27. delve into	深入
28. defective goods	次品
29. trade assurance	信用保证

Exercises

Task 1: Complete the following sentences with the words or phrases in the box.

intermediate	ultimate	alliance	appreciation	approve
surplus	output	status	in essence	delve into

1. Our _____ objective is to have as many female members of parliament as there are male.
2. These documents have no legal _____ in Britain.
3. The companies have formed an _____ to market the product.

4. _____ is up 30% on last year.
5. The conference _____ a proposal for a referendum.
6. _____ his message was very simple.
7. This is a book aiming at students at the _____ level and above.
8. The research _____ this issue deeply.
9. A little bit of currency _____ might help.
10. _____ cash can be invested.

Task 2: Translate the following sentences into Chinese.

1. Supply chain is a network chain structure that connects the supplier, manufacturer, distributor and the final customer. Supply chain starts from kits, then manufactures intermediate and final products.
2. The distribution enterprise is the product circulation agent enterprise aiming at sending the products to every corner of the scope of business.
3. It is a business process about accepting orders, signing contracts, and so forth. The direction of this flow is a two-way flow between supplier and consumer.
4. Its advanced nature lies in its customer and final consumer-oriented ideology as well as manufacturing and supplying mode based on meeting the ultimate requirements of customers and consumers.
5. Finally, it forms an extremely competitive strategic alliance and a whole network structure connecting customer, supplier, manufacturer, seller, service provider and all the other cooperation partners.

Learning Aims Achievement and Test

Section	ERP and Supply Chain of Cross-border E-commerce		Class hours		Course Credit	
Level	Medium	Capability	Be able to talk in English about the basic information covered in this unit concerning ERP and supply chain Be able to identify the key factors in choosing an effective ERP platform Be able to identify the key factors in choosing an effective supply chain platform		Subtask	4
Number	Contents		Criteria			Score

续表

	1	basic concept	Be able to talk in English about the basic information covered in this unit concerning ERP and supply chain	
	2	ERP	Be able to acquire the basic knowledge about the concept, advantages, features and different modules of ERP	
	3	Supply chain and supply chain management	Be able to acquire the basic knowledge about the concept, functions, basic elements and flows of supply chain as well as supply chain management and its advantages	
	4	Cross-border E-commerce ERP and supply chain platforms	Be able to identify the key factors in choosing an effective ERP platform and supply chain platform	
Test and Comments		Score(1 point for each section)		
		Tutor Comments:		

Task Fulfillment Report

Title				
Class		Name		Student ID
Task Fulfillment Report				

1. Present your task and your plan for it.
2. Present the difficulties you came across on completing the task and your solutions.
3. Present what you have learnt through all this process.

Write a report with no less than 200 words.

	Scoring Criteria(10-score range)	
Tutor comments：	Attitude	
	Task Amount	
Scoring Rules		

1. Timely finish all tasks.
2. Finish the tasks in reasonable way.
3. Reliable, coherent, logical and intelligible report.
4. Unfinished task will lead to 1 point deduction, and copy to 5 points deduction.

Keys

Text A

Task 1:

1. recruitment   2. reliable   3. storage   4. conducive   5. rational
6. procurement   7. surpassed   8. evolves from   9. assets   10. orientation

Task 2:

1. 它将企业的人、财、物、产、供应和配送与相关的物流、信息流、资金流、管理流和增值流紧密结合,以此实现资源的优化和共享。

2. ERP超越了传统企业的限制,从供应链范围和现代企业的运营模式方面优化了企业的资源。

3. 它协调了企业的各个管理部门，并按照市场导向组织商业活动。

4. 它采用模块化设计，使得系统本身能够根据企业的需求支持并合并新的模块，以此提升企业的应变能力。

5. 分销管理模块主要管理和统计产品、地区和客户等信息，它也会分析销售量、销售额、利润、评估、消费者等。

Text B

Task 1：

1. ultimate   2. status   3. alliance   4. output   5. approves
6. In essence   7. intermediate   8. delves into   9. appreciation   10. Surplus

Task 2：

1. 供应链具有连接供应商、制造商、分销商和最终客户的网络链条结构。供应链始于配套设备，然后它利用这些配套设备生产出中间产品和最终成品。

2. 分销企业是产品流通代理企业，旨在将产品发往业务范围内的各个角落。

3. 它是关于接受订单、签订合同等的商业流程。这种流程是供应商和消费者之间的双向流通。

4. 它的先进性在于以消费者和最终消费者为中心的理念。同时，其先进性也体现在它是一种基于满足客户和消费者最终需求的生产和供应模式。

5. 最后，它形成了一种极具竞争力的战略联盟，并且是连接了消费者、供应商、生产商、卖家、服务提供商和所有其他合作伙伴的完整网络结构。

参 考 文 献

[1] 阿里巴巴(中国)网络技术有限公司.从0开始跨境电商实训[M].北京:电子工业出版社,2021.
[2] 丁辉,赵岑岑,等.跨境电商多平台运营实战基础[M].北京:电子工业出版社,2020.
[3] 冯晓宁,梁永创,等.跨境电商阿里巴巴速卖通实操全攻略[M].北京:人民邮电出版社,2015.
[4] 京东大学电商学院.京东平台店铺运营[M].2版.北京:电子工业出版社,2021.
[5] 李颖,胡乔立.跨境电商英语教程[M].北京:外语教学与研究出版社,2020.
[6] 王琼.跨境电商实用英语[M].北京:中国人民大学出版社,2018.
[7] 魏家波.亚马逊跨境电商运营宝典[M].北京:电子工业出版社,2018.
[8] 易静,柯可,等.跨境电子商务英语[M].北京:人民邮电出版社,2020.
[9] 张爱强,司爱侠,等.跨境电子商务英语[M].北京:人民邮电出版社,2020.
[10] 纵雨果.亚马逊跨境电商运营——从入门到精通(畅销版)[M].北京:电子工业出版社,2021.

图书资源支持

感谢您一直以来对清华版图书的支持和爱护。为了配合本书的使用,本书提供配套的资源,有需求的读者请扫描下方的"书圈"微信公众号二维码,在图书专区下载,也可以拨打电话或发送电子邮件咨询。

如果您在使用本书的过程中遇到了什么问题,或者有相关图书出版计划,也请您发邮件告诉我们,以便我们更好地为您服务。

我们的联系方式:

地　　址:北京市海淀区双清路学研大厦 A 座 714

邮　　编:100084

电　　话:010-83470236　010-83470237

客服邮箱:2301891038@qq.com

QQ: 2301891038（请写明您的单位和姓名）

资源下载:关注公众号"书圈"下载配套资源。

书 圈

清华计算机学堂

观看课程直播